The

THERAPIST'S

NEWSLETTER

KIT

The
THERAPIST'S
NEWSLETTER
KIT

Laurie Cope Grand

John Wiley & Sons, Inc.

Library of Congress Cataloging-in-Publication Data:

Grand, Laurie Cope.
    The therapist's newsletter kit/Laurie Cope Grand.
        p. cm.
    ISBN 0-471-41339-9 (paper : alk. paper)
    1. Psychotherapy—Authorship. 2. Mental health—Authorship. 3. Newsletters—Publishing. I. Title.

RC437.2 .G73 2001
616.89'14—dc21   2001026443

Printed in the United States of America.

10 9 8 7 6 5 4 3 2

Contents

Contents

Acknowledgments

I am grateful to Kelly Franklin and Tracey Belmont at John Wiley & Sons for their support of this project. I also wish to acknowledge my dear husband, Mark, who will always be my partner in life, my sparkling daughter, Lisa, and my mother, Jean Hamilton Cope, who always sets a wonderful example for me. I would also like to honor Walter Lockwood, my first and best writing teacher, who encouraged me to express myself.

The
THERAPIST'S
NEWSLETTER
KIT

Section 1

Introduction to
The Therapist's
Newsletter Kit

Building a mental health practice is a challenge that becomes greater every year as managed care transforms our health care system. *The Therapist's Newsletter Kit* is a new practice-building tool that will make this endeavor more achievable for therapists in solo private practice, as well as for those who work in group practices, clinics, and counseling centers.

The Therapist's Newsletter Kit is a set of ready-to-use newsletters on 50 different topics of current popular interest. This book includes a disk containing the unformatted newsletter content that the reader can copy and paste into a newsletter template, which is also included on the disk. This makes it easy for you to edit and customize the content to meet the needs and interests of various target readers. It is simple to use by therapists with limited computer and formatting skills.

This time-saving book helps mental health professionals build their private practices by distributing interesting, well-written, well-researched newsletters to referral sources as well as to current and past clients. It is also a valuable product for a community mental health center or counseling agency, since the newsletters may be distributed as a public service. Informative newsletters published on a regular basis are an excellent way to reach out to the community. Many therapists say they plan to write and distribute newsletters like these as a marketing tool at some point in the future, but most lack the necessary research time and may also lack the writing skills. This book makes the task easy and convenient. It provides therapists with a powerful tool for marketing their practices in a professional manner.

Why Newsletters Are an Effective Therapy Marketing Technique

Newsletters are a great way to increase your visibility and make yourself more accessible to potential clients and referral sources. Sending a useful, professional newsletter on a regular basis enables you to:

- Reach out to new potential clients and referral sources.
- Stay in touch with current and past clients.
- Bring back past clients.
- Educate people about your area of specialization.
- Provide added value to your counseling services.
- Showcase your knowledge.
- Highlight your skills.
- Enhance your credibility.
- Stimulate referrals.
- Inform readers of facts they may not have known.
- Keep you in the front of people's minds.
- Publicize your practice to the media.
- Network with community businesses and organizations.
- Tie in with information on your web site.

When and How Often to Send Your Newsletters

A regular newsletter should be one part of your overall marketing plan. According to one marketing expert, people begin to remember your marketing message after they have seen it seven to 10 times. This means that you have to repeat your message and be sure that people see it in more than one place. Your newsletter, along with your print and radio ads, flyers, postcards, newspaper coverage, and other media, can be a central part of your marketing message.

Newsletters should be sent on a regular basis to have an impact and to establish recognition. The ideal frequency is between four and 12 times each year. If you can discipline yourself to produce a monthly newsletter, and can afford the mailing and production costs, you will soon establish a name for yourself. Bimonthly or quarterly is fine, too. The important thing is to design a plan and stick to it. Starting a newsletter program and stopping after two or three issues only makes you look unprofessional.

When you set up your newsletter plan, it's best to schedule it for the coming year. Identify the topics for each issue, choosing from those in this book or combining two or three to make a customized issue to match the needs and interests of your clients.

Some marketing experts advise that you avoid the months when potential clients are likely to be busy with other activities and are less likely to contact you for counseling services. These months include August, November, and December. On the other hand, you may decide to produce your newsletter at regular intervals. This will steadily build your visibility and name recognition so that when people are ready to seek the services of a mental health professional, they will think of you first.

Your Newsletter's Name

Take some time during your planning process to think of a newsletter title that fits you and your practice. I have given each of the newsletters in this book a different title just to show you some examples. After you have chosen one or two possibilities, ask a few friends, colleagues, or family members for their candid reactions. The name you have chosen may make sense to you, but be sure it sounds inviting and makes sense to others as well.

As I was preparing this book, I showed the final manuscript to my teenage daughter, Lisa. She looked at the first page, a newsletter on ideas for writing in one's journal. I had named the newsletter *M.H. News,* a name that made perfect sense to me. (*M.H.,* of course, stands for Mental Health.) She asked, "What does M.H. mean?"

I changed the name. If she was confused, it is likely that others will be as well. It pays to get some feedback before you go public.

Developing Your Mailing List

You may already have a mailing list if you work for a counseling center or group practice. For those of you who are just starting to market your services or who are on your own, there are several places to begin. If you are a member of your local Chamber of Commerce, you can most likely purchase mailing labels for all or some of the members for a few dollars. Other organizations, clubs, and professional associations may offer the same service. You can also build your own list by going through your local Yellow Pages and the directories of organizations you may belong to. Add the names and business addresses of those who may be potential clients or referral sources. Be sure to include businesses and professionals who specialize in areas where your clients are likely to be found. For example, if you specialize in working with children, the names of day care providers, nursery schools, pediatricians, and children's clothing stores should be on your list.

If at all possible, build and maintain your mailing list on your computer. Microsoft® Works, which comes loaded on many computers today and is inexpensive to purchase, has a very simple-to-use database tool that will help you to manage your mailing list. You can easily update it and print address labels each time you have a new issue.

Another option, if you have the budget, is to contact a mailing list broker and purchase a list that is targeted to the demographics of your specific target client. This can be expensive, but it can also be quite effective.

Measuring the Effectiveness of Your Newsletters

It is difficult to precisely measure the effectiveness of a marketing effort, especially when it is for a small business or individual private practice. However, there are a few things you can do to evaluate the impact of your newsletter.

When a new client contacts you for the first time, always ask how he or she heard about you. Keep track of these responses and determine which of your marketing efforts are producing your clients.

You may also wish to include an offer for a free consultation or a discount on ongoing sessions. Keeping track of the responses to these offers is another way of determining the effectiveness of your campaign.

Even if you are unable to identify any clients who came to you directly from your newsletter campaign, this doesn't mean it is not a success. In the mental health business, it takes several years to build a reputation and name recognition. Your newsletter should be just one part of a larger effort designed to let people know who you are and how you can help them.

How to Set Up Your Newsletter Documents

The newsletters in this book are designed in Microsoft® Word. The text of all 58 newsletters is included on the CD-ROM in the back of the book. Each newsletter is a separate file. You will also find a file called Template.doc. This file contains the basic design of the newsletter. These are the steps to follow:

1. Copy all of the files to your hard drive. Don't work from the CD-ROM.
2. Open the Template.doc file.

3. Click File, Save As, and give your first newsletter a name. Let's say you'll call it Newsletter1.doc.

4. Click View, Header and Footer. Replace the name of the newsletter and the other information in the header and footer with your own.

5. Close the header and footer.

6. Save your document.

7. Open the file of the newsletter you want to work on.

8. Select all of the text by clicking Edit, Select All, or by typing Control A.

9. Copy the entire text of the newsletter by clicking Edit, Copy, or by typing Control C.

10. Return to Newsletter1.doc. Put your cursor on the line below the title of the newsletter and paste the text of the newsletter you have just copied. Do this by clicking Edit, Paste, or by typing Control V. The text is now pasted into the newsletter.

11. Save the document.

12. Select the text of the *Title* of the newsletter. Type the actual title you want to replace the sample text.

13. Save the document.

14. The newsletters in this book are designed to have three pages of text and a back page that shows on the outside when folded for mailing.

15. The newsletters are of varying lengths. You may need to make the font smaller or larger to fill up three pages of the newsletter. You can also insert graphics and text boxes to make the pages look more interesting.

16. Follow the same steps to open the document that will serve as your newsletter's back page. The template of the back page is called Backpage.doc.

17. Open Backpage.doc.

18. Click File, Save As, and enter a new name such as backpage1.doc.

19. Click the text boxes and replace the back-page information with your own data.

20. Save the document.

For some excellent ideas on how to give your newsletters sparkle, consider purchasing *Marketing with Newsletters* (second edition) by Elaine Floyd (St. Louis, MO: Newsletter Resources, 1997). This book offers hundreds of tips on how to design and market a newsletter.

Producing and Sending Your Newsletter

It can be quite inexpensive to produce and send a newsletter on a regular basis. The more you can do yourself, the less it will cost you. If you are fairly skilled at using your computer, you can

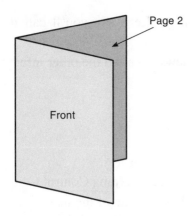

Page 2

Front

produce your newsletter yourself and won't need to pay someone else to do it.

The newsletters in this book will look best if they are printed on 11 × 17 paper and folded in half as shown. The mailing information is printed on page four and the newsletter is folded again in half, with the mailing information on the outside.

When you prepare your newsletters for mailing, close them with tape or a round sticker, not with a staple. Staples make your newsletter more difficult to open and don't look as nice as a round sticker. The U.S. Postal Service allows you to use staples. Visit www.USPS.com for specific information.

Make These Newsletters Your Own

You can use the content of the newsletters in this book in any way you wish. It is not necessary to cite the author of this book. You may use this information as if you wrote it yourself. However, where the work of another author is cited, please be sure to give credit to that author when you use it.

I have designed the content for you to use in your counseling practice. Please feel free to make it your own. If you want to reword, reformat, edit, delete, or add your own opinions and examples, you are free to do that. If you don't like, or disagree with, anything in any newsletter, please change it to suit your own preferences. These newsletters are intended to make it easy for you to get started in your marketing campaign without starting from zero. You may use them exactly as they are written, or you may perform major surgery.

I hope you will find this book useful and that you enjoy marketing your practice with newsletters. If you have any questions, feedback, or suggestions, you can send e-mail to Laurie@LaurieGrand.com. I will be happy to answer your newsletter questions via e-mail and would appreciate hearing your success stories.

Section 2

Sample Newsletters

Mental Health Monitor

1. 33 Ways to Use Your Journal for Self-Discovery and Self-Expression

By Joni McIntyre, MSW

 As a therapist, I often suggest to clients that they explore their feelings and thoughts by keeping a journal. Sometimes clients ask for a bit of direction with this process. Here are some journaling ideas if you're not sure where to start:

1. Write down what happened today and how you felt about it.

2. Write a letter to a person you are angry with. Say everything you are feeling and wish you had the nerve to say.

3. Draw a picture of the person you wrote the letter to in #2.

4. Make a list of all the things you are grateful for. List all the big things, all the small things, and everything in between that you can think of.

5. Circle the three most important things on the list you made in #4. Write a paragraph for each, expressing your appreciation to the person who had the most influence over it. If possible, turn this into an actual letter and send it.

6. Make a list of the things that you feel upset about right now. Write down as many as you can think of until you can't think of any more. Then choose the top five.

7. For each of the top five things you identified in #6, list 10 things you can do to gain control of the situation. Circle the top three from each list.

8. Make a timeline that represents your life. Fill it in with the most significant events that have shaped you: your early years, your teen years, and each decade that has followed. Draw pictures or icons next to the most important events. Use crayons or markers if you wish.

9. Write a few pages about your feelings about the timeline.

10. Describe how your life would be different if _____ had or had not happened. Here are some examples:
    a. If your parents had divorced
    b. If your parents had remained married
    c. If your parents had been married
    d. If your mother hadn't passed away
    e. If you hadn't moved to _____
    f. If you had gone to college

g. If you hadn't gone to college

h. If you had gone to _____ College

i. If you had never met _____

j. If you hadn't broken up
with _____

11. Make a list of all the things you wish you could do before your life is over.

12. Make a list of the things no one knows about you.

13. Write about your junior year in high school.

14. Write about what life was like before you became a parent.

15. Write about what you wish you had known before you became a parent.

16. Make a list of the things you still want to learn about being a parent.

17. Describe what it was like when you first met your partner.

18. Write about what you wish you had known about your partner before you married him/her.

19. Write about what you wish your partner had known about you before (s)he married you.

20. Write a letter to yourself as you were at age 10. Tell yourself:

    a. What your life is like now

    b. What you have learned since you were 10

    c. What you want him or her to know

d. What you want him or her to beware of

e. What you want him or her to enjoy every moment of

21. Write a letter to your own parents. Tell them what your life is like now.

22. Write a letter to someone from your childhood or adolescence who didn't appreciate you or who misunderstood you. Tell the person what you want them to know and how you feel about the lack of connection between you.

23. Think of someone you never acknowledged for something important. Write that person a letter and acknowledge him or her.

24. Think of someone who never acknowledged *you* for something important. Write them a letter and tell them what you want them to know.

25. Make a list of five miracles you want to happen in the coming year. Write a paragraph or two describing each one and how your life will be better if it happens.

26. For each of the five miracles, make a list of:

    a. Five barriers or forces that block or prevent it from happening

    b. Five positive influences, things that encourage or support its happening

    c. Five things you can do to reduce the barriers and strengthen the positive influences

27. Write about the five things you most like to do.

28. Write about the five things you most dislike doing.

29. Make a list of five places you'd like to visit. Describe what you imagine them to be like.

30. Write about three things you most regret doing or not doing. Describe what happened and how you feel about it.

31. Write a letter to your children, even if they have not yet been born. Tell them what you want them to know about you.

32. Write a letter to your grandchildren, even if they have not yet been born. Tell them what you want them to know about you.

33. Write a letter to your descendants one hundred years from now. Describe what your life is like today.

34. Add your own ideas here:

_____

_____

_____

_____

_____

_____

_____

_____

Joni McIntyre is a licensed counselor in Manchester. She specializes in grief therapy and offers groups for people who have lost friends, family members, and pets. Call 555-0987 for your free consultation.

Monthly Informer

2. Addiction: How to Recognize It and What to Do about It

By Faye Springs, Ph.D.

Addiction to alcohol and other drugs is a chronic disease. It is progressive, continuous, and long-term. Alcohol or drug abuse means that a person has control over whether he or she drinks or uses. Alcohol or drug dependence means that a person has lost all control over his or her drinking or using behavior.

Addictive Behavior

People who suffer from addictive diseases engage in compulsive behavior and gradually lose control of their lives. They continue to drink or use drugs, even when they know it will lead to negative consequences. They tend to have low self-esteem and almost inevitably suffer from anxiety and depression.

If someone in your life suffers from addictive disease, you have experienced his or her extreme behavior, ranging from depression to exhilaration. You probably have also experienced the person's state of denial ("I can quit anytime" or "I don't have a problem"), dishonesty, frequent disappointments, and the series of ruined relationships. These are the hallmark behaviors when a person suffers from addiction to alcohol or drugs.

Who Is Affected by Addictive Disease

Alcoholism and drug addiction affect people from all parts of society. Addictive disease affects rock stars, writers, artists, and homeless people. Victims also include stay-at-home moms, teenagers, and corporate executives. There are addicts who are students at top universities and physicians in your local hospital. They may be teachers at your neighborhood school or salespeople at the local hardware store.

Studies have shown that there is a genetic predisposition to alcoholism. About half of all alcoholics had an alcoholic parent. Men seem to be more vulnerable than women to the alcoholic traits of their parents. Women may be more affected by factors in the environment (such as financial and life circumstances) than by inherited factors.

The Physical Side of Addiction

Chronic alcohol abuse produces long-lasting damage in many areas of brain function. It damages the capacity for abstract thinking, problem solving, memory, and physical dexterity. It also impairs verbal, visual, and spatial ability. The extent of damage to brain tissue depends on the extent of heavy alcohol abuse. When the drinking stops, a certain amount of healing is possible.

Prescription Drugs

Prescription and illegal drugs with psychoactive side effects target the brain and can change a person's mood. This causes these drugs to be potentially addicting. Some people think that if a doctor has prescribed a drug, it is not addictive. This is not true.

It is important to tell your doctor if you:

- Are an alcoholic (using or in recovery)
- Have ever been addicted to any drug
- Have taken more than the prescribed dose of a prescribed drug
- Have taken a prescribed drug for a long time
- Take a prescribed drug with alcohol

Addictive disease is often progressive and can be fatal. Thankfully, with proper treatment, recovery is possible.

Treatment

The first phase of treatment of addictive disease focuses on the physical effects of alcohol or drug use. This phase can include detoxification or treating life-threatening disorders such as liver failure.

Since addictive disease is primarily a brain disease that results in behavioral symptoms, the main treatment is psychosocial therapy.

Treatment usually focuses on the irrational feelings and distorted thinking that accompany chronic alcohol or drug abuse.

Alcoholism and drug addiction are chronic diseases that require a lifetime recovery plan. Most successful treatment plans include a focus on the 12 steps of Alcoholics Anonymous and involve ongoing, long-term participation in self-help groups. Patients who have been hospitalized for treatment may continue group and individual psychotherapy after they leave the hospital, in addition to attending 12-Step meetings.

Treatment of the Family

Addiction affects every member of the patient's family. As the disease progresses and the patient continues to drink or use, it causes a range of emotional, spiritual, and financial problems for almost everyone involved, including family, friends and coworkers. When the family is ready to begin the recovery process, Al-Anon and Alateen are excellent resources. A qualified family therapist who understands the process of addiction and recovery may also be consulted to work with the family.

What to Do When an Alcoholic or Addict Won't Stop

Sometimes the alcoholic or addict is in such a strong state of denial that the best alternative is to arrange an intervention. This process involves arranging for a professional interventionist to organize a meeting of the family, friends, and employer of the patient. The interventionist helps the group prepare a confrontation that will be followed by the patient entering a treatment center. The patient's family and friends usually write a brief statement describing how the drinking or drug use has affected them. The interventionist and the group then meet with the patient and read their statements to the patient with the guidance of the interventionist. These interventions, when managed by professionals from respected treatment organizations, often result in successful treatment of the addiction.

Please pass this newsletter along to a friend. Or call 555-0987 to request additional copies.

For more information, visit:

www.casacolumbia.org
www.health.org
www.niaa.nih.gov

Faye Springs is a licensed psychologist in Baker's Lake. She specializes in addictions and codependency. Call 555-0987 for your free consultation.

A Complimentary Newsletter From Fran Kooistra, Ph.D.—Licensed Psychologist

FRAN'S LETTER

3. Why Am I So Anxious?

By Fran Kooistra, Ph.D.

Every human feels anxiety on occasion; it is a part of life. All of us know what it is like to feel worry, nervousness, fear, and concern. We feel nervous when we have to give a speech, go for a job interview, or walk into our boss's office for the annual performance appraisal. We know it's normal to feel a surge of fear when we unexpectedly see a photo of a snake or look down from the top of a tall building. Most of us manage these kinds of anxious feelings fairly well and are able to carry on with our lives without much difficulty. These feelings don't disrupt our lives.

But millions of people (an estimated 15% of the population) suffer from devastating and constant anxiety that severely affects their lives, sometimes resulting in living in highly restricted ways. These people experience panic attacks, phobias, extreme shyness, obsessive thoughts, and compulsive behaviors. The feeling of anxiety is a constant and dominating force that disrupts their lives. Some become prisoners in their own homes, unable to leave to work, drive, or visit the grocery store. For these people, anxiety is much more than just an occasional wave of apprehension.

Types of Anxiety Disorders

An anxiety disorder affects a person's behavior, thoughts, feelings, and physical sensations. The most common anxiety disorders include the following:

Social anxiety or **social phobia** is a fear of being around other people. People who suffer from this disorder always feel self-conscious around others. They have the feeling that everyone is watching them and staring at them, being critical in some way. Because the anxiety is so painful, they learn to stay away from social situations and avoid other people. Some eventually need to be alone at all times, in a room with the door closed. The feeling is pervasive and constant and even happens with people they know.

People who have social anxiety know that their thoughts and fears are not rational. They are aware that others are not actually judging or evaluating them at every moment. But this knowledge does not make the feelings disappear.

Panic disorder is a condition where a person has panic attacks without warning. According to the National Institutes of Mental Health, about 5% of the adult American population suffers from panic attacks. Some experts say that this number is actually higher, since many people experience panic attacks but never receive treatment.

Common symptoms of panic include:

- Racing or pounding heart
- Trembling
- Sweaty palms

- Feelings of terror
- Chest pains or heaviness in the chest
- Dizziness and lightheadedness
- Fear of dying
- Fear of going crazy
- Fear of losing control
- Feeling unable to catch one's breath
- Tingling in the hands, feet, legs, or arms

A panic attack typically lasts several minutes and is extremely upsetting and frightening. In some cases, panic attacks last longer than a few minutes or strike several times in a short time period.

A panic attack is often followed by feelings of depression and helplessness. Most people who have experienced panic say that the greatest fear is that the panic attack will happen again.

Many times, the person who has a panic attack doesn't know what caused it. It seems to have come "out of the blue." At other times, people report that they were feeling extreme stress or had encountered difficult times and weren't surprised that they had a panic attack.

Generalized anxiety disorder is quite common, affecting an estimated 3 to 4% of the population. This disorder fills a person's life with worry, anxiety, and fear. People who have this disorder are always thinking and dwelling on the "what ifs" of every situation. It feels like there is no way out of the vicious cycle of anxiety and worry. The person often becomes depressed about life and their inability to stop worrying.

People who have generalized anxiety usually do not avoid situations, and they don't generally have panic attacks. They can become incapacitated by an inability to shut the mind off, and are overcome with feelings of worry, dread, fatigue, and a loss of interest in life. The person usually realizes these feelings are irrational, but the feelings are also very real. The person's mood can change from day to day, or even hour to hour. Feelings of anxiety and mood swings become a pattern that severely disrupts the quality of life.

People with generalized anxiety disorder often have physical symptoms including headaches, irritability, frustration, trembling, inability to concentrate, and sleep disturbances. They may also have symptoms of social phobia and panic disorder.

Other types of anxiety disorders include:

Phobia, fearing a specific object or situation.

Obsessive-compulsive disorder (OCD), a system of ritualized behaviors or obsessions that are driven by anxious thoughts.

Post-traumatic stress disorder (PTSD), severe anxiety that is triggered by memories of a past traumatic experience.

Agoraphobia, disabling fear that prevents one from leaving home or another safe place.

Treatment Options

Most people who suffer from anxiety disorders begin to feel better when they receive the proper treatment. It can be difficult to identify the correct treatment, however, because each person's anxiety is caused by a unique set of factors. It can be frustrating for the client when treatment is not immediately successful or takes longer than hoped for. Some clients feel better after a few weeks or months of treatment, while others may need a year or more. If a person has an anxiety disorder in combination with another disorder (such as alcoholism and depression), treatment is more complicated and takes longer.

While a treatment plan must be specifically designed for each individual, there are a number of standard approaches. Mental health professionals who specialize in treating anxiety most often use a combination of the following treatments. There is no single correct approach.

Cognitive Therapy

The client learns how to identify and change unproductive thought patterns by observing his or her feelings and learning to separate realistic from unrealistic thoughts.

Behavior Therapy

This treatment helps the client alter and control unwanted behavior. **Systematic desensitization,** a type of behavior therapy, is often used to help people with phobias and OCD. The client is exposed to anxiety-producing stimuli one small step at a time, gradually increasing his or her tolerance to situations that have produced disabling anxiety.

Relaxation Training

Many people with anxiety disorders benefit from self-hypnosis, guided visualization, and biofeedback. Relaxation training is often part of psychotherapy.

Medication

Antidepressant and antianxiety medications can help restore chemical imbalances that cause symptoms of anxiety. This is an effective treatment for many people, especially in combination with psychotherapy.

The treatment for an anxiety disorder depends on the severity and length of the problem. The client's willingness to actively participate in treatment is also an important factor. When a person with panic is motivated to try new behaviors and practice new skills and techniques, he or she can learn to change the way the brain responds to familiar thoughts and feelings that have previously caused anxiety.

> **Please pass this newsletter along to a friend. Or call 555-0987 to request additional copies.**

Fran Kooistra is a licensed psychologist in Grand Rapids. She specializes in working with people who have anxiety disorders. Call 555-0987 for your free consultation.

EMOTIONS TODAY

4. Assertive Communication: 20 Tips

By Tom Phillips, MSW

Most of us know that assertiveness will get you further in life than being passive or aggressive. But few of us were actually taught **how** to be assertive. Here are some helpful tips.

1. **Choose the right time.** Imagine you're dashing down the hall on your way to a meeting. Lisa passes by. You call out, "Can you have the Microsoft project out by Tuesday?" Because you haven't scheduled a special time to bring up the issue, Lisa has no reason to think your request deserves high priority.

2. **Choose the right place.** Discuss important issues in a private, neutral location.

3. **Be direct.** For example, "Lisa, I would like you to work overtime on the Microsoft project." Whether or not Lisa likes your request, she respects you for your directness.

4. **Say "I," not "we."** Instead of saying, "We need the project by Tuesday," say, "I would like you to finish the project by Tuesday."

5. **Be specific.** Instead of, "Put a rush on the Microsoft project," say, "I would like the Microsoft project finished and on Joe's desk by 9:00 Tuesday morning."

6. **Use body language to emphasize your words.** "Lisa, I need that report Tuesday morning," is an assertive statement. But if you mumble this statement while staring at the floor, you undermine your message.

7. **Confirm your request.** Ask your staff to take notes at meetings. At the end of each meeting, ask your group to repeat back the specifics that were agreed upon. This minimizes miscommunication.

8. **Stand up for yourself.** Don't allow others to take advantage of you; insist on being treated fairly. Here are a few examples: "I was here first," "I'd like more coffee, please," "Excuse me, but I have another appointment," "Please turn

down the radio," or "This steak is well done, but I asked for medium rare."

9. **Learn to be friendly** with people you would like to know better. Do not avoid people because you don't know what to say. Smile at people. Convey that you are happy to see them.

10. **Express your opinions honestly.** When you disagree with someone, do not pretend to agree. When you are asked to do something unreasonable, ask for an explanation.

11. **Share your experiences and opinions.** When you have done something worthwhile, let others know about it.

12. **Learn to accept kind words.** When someone compliments you, say, "Thank you."

13. **Maintain eye contact** when you are in a conversation.

14. **Don't get personal.** When expressing annoyance or criticism, comment on the person's *behavior* rather than attacking the person. For example: "Please don't talk to me that way," rather than, "What kind of jerk are you?"

15. **Use "I" statements** when commenting on another's behavior. For example: "When you cancel social arrangements at the last minute, it's extremely inconvenient and I feel really annoyed."

16. **State what you want.** If appropriate, ask for another behavior. ("I think we'd bet-

ter sit down and try to figure out how we can make plans together and cut down on this kind of problem.")

17. **Look for good examples.** Pay attention to assertive people and model your behavior after theirs.

18. **Start slowly.** Express your assertiveness in low-anxiety situations at first; don't leap into a highly emotional situation until you have more confidence. Most people don't learn new skills overnight.

19. **Reward yourself** each time you push yourself to formulate an assertive response. Do this regardless of the response from the other person.

20. **Don't put yourself down** when you behave passively or aggressively. Instead, identify where you went off course and learn how to improve.

Tom Phillips is a Licensed Clinical Social Worker in St. Louis. He works with individuals, couples and families. He also has several ongoing groups. Call 555-0987 for your free consultation.

Mental Health News

5. Depression: What It Is and What to Do about It (Part I)

By Karen Johnson, Ph.D.

This is the first of a two-part series on depression. In this issue, I will explore what depression is and what causes it. In the next issue, I will describe how depression is treated and prevented. If you or someone close to you suffers from depression, it is important to educate yourself about it and seek treatment from qualified mental health professionals.

Depression is a serious illness, not a harmless part of life. It is a complex disorder with a variety of causes. It is never caused by just one thing. It may be the result of a mix of factors, including genetic, chemical, physical, and sociological. It is also influenced by behavior patterns learned in the family and by cognitive distortions.

Depression affects millions of people in this country. It is always troubling, and for some people it can be disabling. Depression is more than just sadness or "the blues." It can have an impact on nearly every aspect of a person's life. People who suffer from depression may experience despair and worthlessness, and this can have an enormous impact on both personal and professional relationships. In this newsletter, I will describe many of the factors that may cause

depression, and I will explore strategies for preventing it.

Depression Is Pervasive

When a person suffers from depression, it can affect every part of his or her life, including one's physical body, one's behavior, thought processes, mood, ability to relate to others, and general lifestyle.

Symptoms of Depression

People who are diagnosed with clinical depression have a combination of symptoms from the following list:

- Feelings of hopelessness, even when there is reason to be hopeful
- Fatigue or low energy
- Much less interest or pleasure in most regular activities
- Low self-esteem
- Feeling worthless
- Excessive or inappropriate guilt
- Lessened ability to think or concentrate
- Indecisiveness
- Thinking distorted thoughts; having an unrealistic view of life
- Weight loss or gain without dieting
- Change in appetite
- Change in sleeping patterns
- Recurrent thoughts of death
- Suicidal thoughts
- A specific plan for committing suicide

- A suicide attempt
- Feelings of restlessness or being slowed down

When a person is suffering from depression, these symptoms cause significant distress or impairment in social, occupational, or other important areas of functioning. This means that the person's family and social relationships, as well as work life, are impaired.

When a person is suffering from depression, symptoms such as these are *not* the result of a chronic psychotic disorder, substance abuse, general medical condition, or bereavement.

Grief, Sadness, and Depression

Depression may include feelings of sadness, but it is not the same as sadness. Depression lasts much longer than sadness. While depression involves a loss of self-esteem, grief, disappointment and sadness do not. People who are depressed function less productively. People who are sad or disappointed continue to function.

Depression and Socioeconomic Factors

Depression does not seem to be related to ethnicity, education, income, or marital status. It strikes slightly more women than men. Some researchers believe that depression strikes more often in women who have a history of emotional and sexual abuse, economic deprivation, or are dependent on others. There seems to be a genetic link; depression is more common among parents, children, and siblings of people who are

diagnosed with depression. The average age at the onset of a depressive episode is the mid-20s. People born more recently are being diagnosed at a younger age.

Physical Causes

Many physicians believe that depression results from a chemical imbalance in the brain. They often prescribe antidepressant medication, and many people find relief as a result. However, there is no reliable test to identify such a chemical imbalance. It is unknown whether life experiences cause mood changes, which create changes in brain chemistry, or whether it works in reverse.

Depression may be associated with physical events such as other diseases, physical trauma, and hormonal changes. A person who is depressed should always have a physical examination as part of the assessment process to determine the role of physical causes.

Signs That Professional Treatment Is Needed

If you or someone you know is depressed and exhibits any of the following signs, it is extremely important to seek the assistance of a medical or mental health professional.

1. Thinking about death or suicide. This is always dangerous and you should see a professional therapist immediately.
2. When symptoms of depression continue for a long time, you may need professional help. Acute responses to events are normal, but they should not last beyond a reasonable time.

3. Your ability to function is impaired by your depression. Seek help before your life situation deteriorates to a serious level.
4. You have become so isolated that you have no one with whom to check reality. Seek out someone to share your thoughts and feelings with.
5. Depressive symptoms have become severe.

In my next newsletter, I will discuss the treatment and prevention of depression.

Suggested Reading

David D. Burns, M.D., *Feeling Good: The New Mood Therapy.* New York, Avon Books, 1980.

The American Psychiatric Association, *Diagnostic and Statistical Manual, 4th Edition.* Washington, D.C., The American Psychiatric Association, 1994.

Michael Yapko, Ph.D., *Breaking the Patterns of Depression.* New York, Doubleday, 1997.

Karen Johnson is a licensed psychologist in Northridge. She specializes in working with people who have mood disorders. Call 555-0987 for your free consultation.

Mental Health News

6. Depression: What It Is and What to Do about It (Part II)

By Karen Johnson, Ph.D.

This is the second of a two-part series on depression. In this issue, I will describe how depression is treated and prevented. If you or someone close to you suffers from depression, it is important to educate yourself about it and seek treatment from qualified mental health professionals.

There are three basic ways to treat depression: psychotherapy, self-help, and medication. Many people respond best to a combination of two or more methods.

1. **Psychotherapy:** Exploring one's beliefs and ways of thinking, and learning new ways of thinking and behaving, with the guidance of a professional.
2. **Self-help:** Exploring one's beliefs and ways of thinking on one's own.
3. **Medication:** Altering one's brain chemistry by taking antidepressant medication.

A physician may recommend medication when four conditions exist:

1. The patient's depression is severe.
2. The patient has suffered at least two previous depressive episodes.
3. There is a family history of depression.
4. The patient asks for medication only and refuses psychotherapy.

There are four types of antidepressant medication available today:

- Tricyclic antidepressants (TCAs)
- Monoamine oxidase inhibitors (MAOIs)
- Selective serotonin reuptake inhibitors (SSRIs)
- Structurally unrelated compounds

The TCAs and MAOIs have been used for decades. The SSRIs (such as Prozac) and structurally unrelated compounds are newer and are being prescribed more and more frequently. They have fewer and less pronounced side effects than the TCAs and MAOIs.

Treatment without Medicine

One of the leading methods for treating depression is cognitive therapy. Cognitive therapists help depressed clients feel better by identifying how faulty ways of thinking are making him or her feel bad. The client analyzes his or her thoughts and beliefs, and learns to substitute more healthy ways of thinking and believing.

Many mental health professionals believe that the ideal treatment of clinical depression is medication in conjunction with psychotherapy.

Prevention of Depression

Depression can often be prevented. It is especially important to take preventive action if you are aware that you have predisposing factors such as those mentioned in the last newsletter.

1. **Identify your risk factors and be aware of where you are vulnerable.** Each of us has unique risk factors, such as things we were taught in our families of origin, values we have learned, and the presence or absence of a family history of depression. Anything that has been learned can be unlearned and replaced with something healthier.

2. **Learn to manage stress.** You can learn proven techniques for calming and relaxing yourself. Consider taking a stress management class or buying a set of relaxation tapes.

3. **Learn problem-solving skills.** Many people who develop depression never learned problem-solving skills. They need to develop the ability to see problems from many viewpoints and to look for a variety of solutions.

4. **Build your life around things you can control.** Learn to recognize what you can control and what you can't. Avoid spending much effort on situations that won't pay off for you.

5. **Learn self-acceptance.** Instead of rejecting the parts of yourself you don't like, learn to manage them more productively.

6. **Become aware of selective perception.** Observe how you generate ideas and opinions about people and events. Remember that these are just your views, not necessarily objective facts.

7. **Focus on the future, not the past.** Depressed people tend to be focused on the past. People who set goals and focus on the future tend to be more positive about life.

8. **Develop a sense of purpose.** Many depressed people lack a sense of purpose or meaning. This means they have no goals and nothing in the future drawing them forward. To prevent depression, develop your sense of purpose and meaning.

9. **Strengthen your emotional boundaries and set limits.** Boundaries define your role in a social situation. They determine how you will or won't behave in a given situation. Having clear, strong boundaries is empowering, while boundary violations make you feel victimized and helpless. Setting limits means having and enforcing rules for the behaviors you expect in a relationship.

10. **Build positive and healthy relationships.** Think about what you need from others in relationships. Learn to read people and trust your instincts about which people are good for you.

11. **Avoid isolation.** Talk to others about what's going on with you. If you keep your thoughts to yourself, you may be unaware that your thoughts are distorted. If you share them with another person, you can become more objective.

Signs That Professional Therapy Is Needed

1. Thinking about death or suicide. This is always dangerous and you should see a professional therapist immediately.

2. When symptoms of depression continue for a long time, you may need profes-

sional help. Acute responses to events are normal, but they should not last beyond a reasonable time.

3. Your ability to function is impaired by your depression. Seek help before your life situation deteriorates to a serious level.

4. You have become so isolated that you have no one with whom to test reality. Seek someone out to share your thoughts and feelings with.

5. Depressive symptoms have become severe.

Suggested Reading

David D. Burns, M.D., *Feeling Good: The New Mood Therapy.* New York, Avon Books, 1980.

Michael Yapko, Ph.D., *Breaking the Patterns of Depression.* New York, Doubleday, 1997.

Karen Johnson is a licensed psychologist in Northridge. She specializes in working with people who have mood disorders. Call 555-0987 for your free consultation.

Psych Update

7. How People Change

By Kim Chung, M.A.

What Is Happiness?

If you are thinking about changing your life for the better, one way to start is by identifying your goals. You are probably hoping to find some version of happiness or emotional well-being. That might look like any combination of the following:

- A sense of freedom
- Self-esteem
- Self-confidence
- Happy to get up in the morning
- Working toward goals
- A sense of purpose in life
- Satisfying relationships

What Is Unhappiness?

If you are thinking about changing your life, you may be experiencing some combination of the following elements:

- Feeling sad, lethargic or depressed
- Feeling afraid
- Abusing or being addicted to alcohol or drugs
- Feeling lonely
- Anxiety
- Problems with relationships
- Not getting what you want in life; feeling frustrated in working toward goals
- Not caring enough to have goals

How Will *You* Change?

When you decide to change your life, try the following ideas.

1. **Explore your feelings.** Keep a journal, talk to a trusted friend, work with a professional counselor.
2. **Envision your future.** Write in a journal, make a collage, do a guided visualization, talk to a friend or counselor, research the possibilities.
3. **Explore wishes and dreams.** Keep a journal, talk to a trusted friend, work with a professional counselor.
4. **Be open to new ideas.** Take a class, travel, say yes to things you may have avoided in the past.
5. **Look for kindred spirits.** Avoid people who make you feel bad about yourself, seek out those who make you blossom, reach out to those with similar interests and dreams.
6. **Try something different.** Deliberately buy new items, try different brands, shop at different stores, do the opposite of what you usually do, see different movies, read different kinds of books and magazines.

28

7. **Set goals and targets.** Learn how to set useful goals, follow through, evaluate progress regularly, reward yourself for achievement.

8. **Take one step at a time.** Divide your goals into tiny pieces and do one small new thing each day, starting now.

9. **Look for lessons.** Remind yourself that experiences are not good or bad; they are simply lessons.

How to Overcome Your Resistance to Change

Have you ever noticed that when you think about changing your life, you feel resistant? Many people say that they not only feel resistant, but they actually do things to keep their lives familiar. They do things like start a diet and then eat a candy bar on the first day, or quit smoking and then sneak a puff.

There are some things you can do to make yourself less resistant. Here are six effective strategies:

1. **Eliminate clutter.** Clutter can be viewed as a sign of uncertainty. Accumulating "stuff" might be stopping you from committing to an important thing. If you keep a lot of half-started projects around, it makes it difficult to zero in on the really important things.

2. **Start small.** Thinking of your overall goal can be overwhelming. So manage your resistance by choosing one small part of it and attacking it today. Let's say your goal is to lose 20 pounds. That can certainly seem like an impossible thing to accomplish. It will seem more doable if you tell yourself, I'm going to lose five pounds by (date).

3. **Disprove your disempowering beliefs.** In *Reinventing Your Life,* authors Young and Klosko suggest that you identify the beliefs that keep you from succeeding. They offer a way to dispute those beliefs by asking, "Is there really an evidence today that this belief is true?" They suggest making a list of the evidence.

4. **Remind yourself of all of your available options.** You always have alternatives and the power to choose among them.

5. **Take responsibility for what you want.** Look for signs that you are blaming your situation on others or not admitting past mistakes. Acknowledge them and move on.

6. **Visualize the future.** Author Barbara Sher suggests one way to do this: Write an imaginary press release about yourself. The date is today's date, two years in the future. The press release is announcing the most extraordinary event you can think of. It doesn't matter whether this event seems only vaguely possible to you. The important thing is that it is exciting to imagine.

When to Seek Professional Help

Sometimes it makes sense to find a professional counselor to work with as you work through the change process. Here are some ways to know when that would be appropriate:

1. You've tried several things but you still have the problem.

2. You want to find a solution sooner rather than later.
3. You have thoughts of harming yourself or others.
4. You have symptoms of depression, anxiety, or another disorder that are significantly interfering with your daily functioning and the quality of your life. For example, you have lost time from work, your relationships have been harmed, your health is suffering. These are signs that you may need the help of a trained, licensed professional.

Please pass this newsletter along to a friend. Or call 555-0987 to request additional copies.

Suggested Reading

Martha Friedman, *Overcoming the Fear of Success.* New York, Warner Books, 1980.

Susan Jeffers, *Feel the Fear and Do It Anyway.* New York, Fawcett Columbine, 1987.

Barbara Sher, *Live the Life You Love.* New York Delacorte Press, 1996.

Jeffrey Young and Janet Klosko, *Reinventing Your Life: How to Break Free from Negative Life Patterns and Feel Good Again.* New York, Plume Books, 1994.

Kim Chung is a licensed counselor and Executive Director of the South Bay Center. The Center provides affordable mental health services to residents of the South Bay. Call 555-0987 for your free consultation.

Client Newsletter

8. How to Be More Self-Confident

By Cheryl Asher, Center Director

Signs of Self-Confidence

 Let's explore the meaning of self-confidence by taking a quiz. Read the list of statements below and check which ones, in your opinion, are signs of self-confidence.

1. Admitting when you are wrong.
2. Being flexible when change is needed.
3. Talking about your accomplishments.
4. Describing negative events in positive terms. For example, "We didn't make our target, but we sure learned a lot."
5. Dressing to please yourself without worrying what others will think.
6. Using a strong handshake.
7. Using casual language in an effort to avoid sounding too "corporate." For example, "You guys did a cool thing."
8. Speaking very fast.
9. Smiling often.
10. Learning new skills.
11. Putting yourself down in order to sound humble.

Compare your answers to those on the bottom of page three under "Quiz #1."

Low Self-Confidence

Part of defining self-confidence is thinking about what *low* self-confidence is, what it looks and sounds like. Test yourself now. Circle the statements that convey a *lack* of self-confidence.

1. "I may be wrong, but I think the answer is ten."
2. "Thank you for the compliment. We're very proud of our work."
3. "That was really stupid of me."
4. "I forgot my business cards. I left them in the car."
5. (Responding to a compliment) "Oh, I've had this dress for ten years."
6. "I would have gotten into the program, but they don't like to take people with my background."
7. "That sounds like a challenge. I'm sure we can figure out how to solve it, though."
8. "I'm sorry to interrupt, but I wonder if I could have a minute of your time."

Compare your answers to those listed at the bottom of page three under "Quiz #2."

Where Does Self-Confidence Come From?

Self-confidence is not something people are born with. It results from a combination of factors:

1. **Learned skill:** Self-confidence is a combination of skills, not just a single qual-

ity. People are *not* born with it or without it. It can be learned.

2. **Practice:** Self-confidence comes from practice. It may appear to be spontaneous, but it isn't.

3. **Internal locus of control:** Self-confidence results from what psychologists call an internal locus (central point) of control. This means that people who are self-directing, who accept responsibility for their own results, have greater self-confidence.

8 Self-Confidence Builders

There are many concrete, specific things you can do to feel more confident in challenging life situations. Make note of those that will help you develop your own sense of self-confidence.

1. **Follow your strengths.** Self-confidence comes from being the best "you" possible. It doesn't come from trying to be someone else. It is the result of following paths like these:

   • Do what comes naturally.
   • Develop your talents.
   • Follow your convictions.
   • Express your own style.

2. **Plan ahead.** Many people are surprised to hear that self-confidence comes from something as ordinary as planning. But think about it; let's say you are going on a job interview, almost always an anxiety-producing experience. When you are prepared, you feel more confident.

3. **Take action.** Confidence comes from taking action. Break your challenge down into small steps and take that first step, no matter how small it seems.

4. **Study.** The more you know about your subject, the more confident you will feel. In fact, the lack of self-confidence almost always stems from a lack of information. We've all had that sick feeling that we don't fully understand what we are talking about.

5. **Act the part.** The following tips will help you begin to present yourself in a positive way.

   • Find a role model. Look for someone who is already successful in your field. Observe him or her and identify for yourself what behaviors convey self-confidence.

   • Look and act powerful. Watch people who create a powerful impression. It could be a TV anchor, a character in a movie, or a coworker. Imagine yourself behaving in a similar way. For an example, watch the movie *Top Hat.* Fred Astaire exudes confidence.

   • Be aware of nonverbal behavior that detracts from presenting yourself with confidence. Ask for feedback from a trusted friend or watch yourself on videotape.

6. **Rehearse for success.** One of the most important ways to boost your self-confidence is by rehearsing important conversations and presentations. You can never be too prepared. These ideas will help you practice so that you really understand your subject:

   • *Manage your anxiety.* Feeling anxious is normal when you are in a challenging situation. The key is learning to manage anxiety so it doesn't paralyze you or diminish your effectiveness.

- *Get organized.* When your materials are prepared and well-organized, you will feel better about your ability to access them. Having information scattered in too many places makes you feel out of control and undermines your self-confidence.

7. **Persist.** Self-confidence is the result of a lot of hard work. The process takes time.

It has been said that success is 99% persistence and 1% talent.

8. **Enjoy your success.** When you reach your goal, don't forget to give yourself credit for working hard. Be proud of what you've accomplished. Here are some ways you can do this:

- Look in the mirror and say to yourself, "Good work. I'm proud of you."
- Think of a way to reward yourself.
- Tell others about your success.
- Write yourself a letter or explore your accomplishment in your journal.
- Draw a picture expressing your achievement.

Answers to Quiz #1

Items 1, 2, 3, 4, 6, 9, and 10 are generally signs of *self-confidence.* The others could be seen as self-sabotaging behaviors.

Answers to Quiz #2

Items 1, 3, 4, 5, 6, and 8 communicate *low* self-confidence. (Of course, there are no 100% right answers, since many of the statements depend on context, tone of voice, cultural interpretation, and other factors.)

Suggested Reading

Barbara De Angelis, *Confidence: Finding It and Living It.* Carson, CA: Hay House, 1995.

Andrew J. DuBrin, *Stand Out: 330 Ways for Gaining the Edge With Bosses, CoWorkers, Subordinates and Customers.* Englewood Cliffs, NJ: Prentice Hall, 1993.

Gene Garofalo, *Hit the Ground Running: Winning Secrets for Keeping Your Career On Track and Moving Forward.* Englewood Cliffs, NJ: Prentice Hall, 1993.

Barbara Sher with Annie Gottlieb, *Wishcraft: How to Get What You Really Want.* New York: Ballantine Books, 1979.

The Center for Mental Health has served the West Valley since 1976. Call 555-0987 for your free consultation.

The Counselor

9. How to Have More Self-Esteem

By Rudy Burger, Ph.D

What Is Self-Esteem?

 Self-esteem literally means to esteem, or respect, yourself. Having high self-esteem means that you have a positive image of yourself. Let's look at where such a positive self-image comes from.

In her classic book *Celebrate Yourself,* Dorothy Corkville Briggs makes a distinction between the real you and your self-image. She says that the *real* you is unique and unchanging. Most of your self-image—what you think is true about yourself—is learned. It is not necessarily accurate at all!

Where are your beliefs about yourself drawn from? Where did you learn them? If you think about it, you'll see that they came from:

- What others said about you
- What others told you
- What others did to you

Your self-image is the result of all the messages you heard about yourself as a child. These messages added up to a set of beliefs about who you are. It may have nothing to do with who you *really* are.

For example, you may believe things like:

- I'm not very smart.
- I'm naturally passive.
- Girls aren't any good at math.
- I'm too old to start over.
- All of the women in the Breski family become doctors.
- I'm painfully shy.
- The Hurleys never lie.

In addition to learning to believe certain things during our early years, there are certain situations that make most people feel inferior or lacking in self-esteem.

Some examples are:

- Being criticized
- Not being loved
- Being rejected
- Experiencing failure

What Low Self-Esteem Feels Like

In situations like these above, it is not uncommon to feel emotions such as:

- Sadness
- Inferiority
- Anger

- Jealousy
- Rejection

Cognitive Therapy

Cognitive therapy is one of the most successful methods for helping people feel better about themselves. Cognitive therapists help depressed and anxious people feel better by identifying how faulty ways of thinking are making them feel bad. They believe that faulty thoughts cause us to feel bad, which makes us feel bad about ourselves.

Cognitive therapists call these faulty ways of thinking "twisted thinking." Cognitive therapy is a process where the client analyzes his or her thoughts and beliefs, and learns to substitute more healthy ways of thinking and believing. These therapists help their clients feel better in four steps: First, identify the upsetting events that cause bad feelings; second, record your thoughts about the event; third, identify the distortions in your thinking process; and fourth, substitute rational responses. When the client successfully completes these four steps, the client usually feels better about him- or herself.

Thinking the right kinds of thoughts is one way to feel good about yourself. Now let's talk about a second way to increase your self-esteem: by taking a look at your life environment and seeing whether it supports you feeling good about yourself. You may find that some nourishing elements need to be replenished. Here are some questions to ask yourself:

Do you have people in your life who:

1. Treat you with love and respect?

2. Encourage you to do and be anything you want?

3. Help you find out what you want to do, and how to do it?

4. Encourage you to explore all of your talents and interests?

5. Are thrilled when you succeed?

6. Listen to you when you need to complain?

7. Help you bounce back from failure without making you feel bad?

Take a moment to think about each of the items on this list. Note where your environment is providing adequately for you, and where it is lacking. This can give you clues to how to build your own self-esteem.

Strategies for Esteem Building

1. Pay attention to how you are feeling from moment to moment. Tune in to what your five senses are experiencing. Take it down to the most basic level of "I feel warm right now," "I feel light-headed," "I feel a tightness in my stomach."

2. Revisit your interests and goals. Make a list of things you'd like to do and learn. Today, take one step toward learning more.

3. Spend less time with critical people and more time with those who appreciate you.

4. Spend some time with yourself at the end of each day. Review what happened

and how you were feeling. Write about it in a private journal.

5. If you are feeling bad about yourself, consider finding a therapist to help you get your life on a positive track.

Please pass this newsletter along to a friend. Or call 555-0987 to request additional copies.

Suggested Reading

Nathaniel Branden, *The Six Pillars of Self-Esteem.* New York, Bantam, 1994.

Dorothy Corkville Briggs, *Celebrate Your Self: Making Life Work For You.* Garden City, NY: Doubleday, 1977.

David D. Burns, *Ten Days to Self-Esteem.* New York, William Morrow, 1993.

Barbara Sher with Annie Gottlieb, *Wishcraft.* New York, Ballantine Books, 1979.

Rudy Burger is a licensed psychologist in West Ensley. She specializes in working with families and teens. Call 555-0987 for your free consultation.

The Real Issues

10. When Should You Consult a Mental Health Professional?

By Samantha Boyd, M.A.

Most of us experience times when we need help to deal with problems and issues that cause us emotional distress. When you are having a problem or dilemma that is making you feel overwhelmed, you may benefit from the assistance of an experienced, trained professional. Professional counselors and therapists offer the caring, expert assistance that people need during stressful times.

There are many types of mental health providers to choose from. The most important thing is to select a licensed professional who has the appropriate training and qualifications to help a person with your specific issues. You should also choose someone with whom you can feel comfortable enough to speak freely and openly.

Types of Problems

People seek the assistance of a mental health professional (MHP) for many different reasons. These are some of the most common:

1. You feel unhappy most of the time.
2. You worry all the time and are unable to find the solutions to your problems.
3. You feel extremely sad and helpless.
4. You feel nervous, anxious, and worried most of the time.
5. You have panic attacks.
6. You have a hard time concentrating.
7. Your emotional state is affecting your daily life: your sleep, eating habits, job, and relationships.
8. You are having a hard time functioning from day to day. Your emotional state is affecting your performance at work or school.
9. Your behavior is harmful to yourself or to others.
10. You are feeling impatient and angry with someone you are taking care of.
11. You are having problems with your family members or in other important relationships.
12. You or someone you care about has problems with substance abuse or other addictions.
13. You are the victim of sexual abuse or domestic violence.
14. You have an eating disorder.
15. You are having trouble getting over the death of someone you loved.

16. You or someone you love has a serious illness and you are having a hard time with it.
17. You feel lonely and isolated.
18. You are experiencing problems in a sexual relationship.
19. Your family has a lot of conflict and tension.
20. You are experiencing a divorce or marital separation.
21. You are having a hard time coping with change.
22. You often feel afraid, angry, or guilty.
23. You have a hard time setting and reaching goals.
24. Your child is having problems with behavior or school performance.
25. Your family is stressed because someone is ill.
26. You have a hard time talking with your partner, children, parents, family members, friends, or coworkers.
27. You are having problems dealing with your own sexual orientation or the sexual orientation of someone you care about.
28. You are planning to marry, and you have some concerns.
29. You have gotten a divorce and your family needs help adjusting.
30. You are part of a blended family and need help learning to live together.

Types of Mental Health Professionals

The most common MHPs in the United States are Psychologists, Marriage and Family Therapists, Social Workers, and Professional Counselors. Each state has its own licensing laws and standards that govern each type of professional. While all licensed MHPs can help most people with problems of living, each group has its own special training in specific areas that makes them more qualified for certain types of issues. In addition, each individual therapist has a unique set of experiences that makes him or her uniquely qualified to work with certain kinds of issues.

Psychologists generally have a Ph.D. or Psy.D. degree in psychology from an accredited school. They must complete a rigorous internship period and pass a state licensing exam. In addition to their undergraduate college degree, most psychologists spend five to seven years in education and training. They study scientific methods and the science of human behavior, building skills for working with people who have real life problems.

Marriage and Family Therapists (MFTs) generally have a master's degree in psychology, counseling, or a related subject from an accredited school. In most states, they must complete a supervised internship period and pass a state licensing exam. Marriage and family therapists are trained to work with people, focusing on how they relate to others. While they often work with an individual client, the focus of treatment is the set of relationships that surround the client and how those relationships impact the client. MFTs are trained in psychotherapy and family systems. They are licensed to diagnose and treat mental and emotional disorders within the context of marriage, couples, and family systems. They work in a variety of settings with individuals, couples, families, children and adolescents, providing support and a fresh viewpoint as people struggle with life's challenges.

Social Workers have a BSW or MSW from an accredited school. They must have completed an MSW and a supervised internship before passing a state licensing exam. (Each state has its own licensing regulations.)

The social work profession focuses on individual happiness and well-being in a social context. It is also concerned with the well-being of the society that surrounds the individual. Social workers are trained to pay attention to the environmental forces that may contribute to the individual's life problems.

Licensed Counselors have a master's degree in psychology or a related subject from an accredited school. In most states, they must complete a supervised internship period and pass a state licensing exam.

Referral to Other Health Professionals

When it is in the best interest of the patient or outside the scope of the MHP's license, therapists collaborate with and refer to other health professionals, such as physicians or psychiatrists in the case of prescribing medication.

Confidentiality

Each group of MHPs has strict ethical guidelines governing privacy and confidentiality. Clients of licensed MHPs can expect that discussions will be kept confidential, except as otherwise required or permitted by law. Examples of times when confidentiality must be broken are when child abuse has occurred or where the client threatens violence against another person.

When you are looking for a mental health professional to help you address your issues, it is very important to ask about a therapist's qualifications to treat your specific concerns.

Please pass this newsletter along to a friend. Or call 555-0987 to request additional copies.

Visit these web sites to learn more:

www.aamft.org (National Association of Marriage and Family Therapy)

www.apa.org (American Psychological Association)

www.naswdc.org (National Association of Social Work)

www.counseling.org (American Counseling Association)

Samantha Boyd is a licensed counselor and Clinical Director of the Family Therapy Center in Salem. Call 555-0987 for your free consultation.

Emotional Wellness Letter

11. Dealing with Midlife Issues

By Arnie Graham, M.A.

In this month's newsletter, I would like to help you explore the challenges and opportunities that come at midlife. You will have an opportunity to take a look at issues that are specific to the Baby Boomer generation. You will also have a chance to begin the process of your own midlife assessment with a list of questions presented at the end of the newsletter. I call this assessment the Midlife Checkup.

Benefits of the Midlife Checkup

Taking the time to assess how your life is going at this point can result in benefits such as these:

- It can help you identify and intensify your inner strengths.
- You can find your own voice and express it your own way.
- You can accept your changing physical self.
- It is an opportunity to forgive those with whom you've been angry.
- It can help you find ways to reduce stress.
- You can learn to simplify your life.
- You can reenergize yourself in preparation for the second half of your life.

The Baby Boomers

The Baby Boomer generation is at midlife right now. This generation includes almost 78 million Americans born between 1946 and 1964.

The Boomers are the largest generation in U.S. history. They have had a major impact on American society as they have passed through every life stage. They are passing through midlife in their own unique way, differently from their parents and differently from Generation X, the group born in the years after 1964.

The first Boomer turned 50 at the beginning of 1996, and the remaining 78 million will observe this anniversary sometime between now and 2014.

Typical Feelings

According to *Rocking the Ages* authors J. Walker Smith and Ann Clurman (researchers at Yankelovich Partners) and authors like Gail Sheehy, people passing through middle age typically experience the following kinds of feelings.

Great expectations: Most Boomers are beginning to recognize their own limitations. Growing up in the comfortable 1950's, the Boomers learned to expect unlimited growth and endless possibilities. They believed their good luck would never end. Now that they are turning 50, many are shocked to discover that there are limits to life's possibilities.

Regret: As people reach midlife, they must face up to the loss of some of their dreams and regret the mistakes they have made. It is not easy for anyone to face the person one will never be.

Loss: At midlife, everyone has to face the loss of beauty and youth, valued by our society. In her book *New Passages,* author Gail Sheehy calls this experience "The Body Blues" or "The Vanity Crisis."

Meaning: According to Sheehy, the "universal preoccupation" of the middle years is "the search for meaning in whatever we do." As they face the fact that time is limited, the Baby Boomers typically become even more intent on this need to analyze and search for significance.

Change: The midlife years can be a time of radical change for many people. This is the result of endless questioning and evaluation of how one has lived life thus far. Many midlife *crises* become mid-life *meltdowns,* says Sheehy, because some people react to feelings of emptiness or disillusionment by destroying everything they have built.

The Boomers developed a value system that is based on a sense of entitlement and which values individuality. Because they hold these values, Boomers respond differently to each life stage than do other generations. You can see these values reflected in scenes like those from television shows from the 1950s and early 60s.

According to Smith and Clurman, four important characteristics of the Baby Boomer value system are:

Self-absorption: The Boomers (once called the "Me" Generation) have the reputation of being more narcissistic than other genera-

tions. Because of the times they grew up in, they have always been fascinated with themselves. The indulgence they experienced at home in the 1950s and the world's seemingly limitless possibilities created a fascination with self and a feeling of specialness.

Sense of entitlement: As a generation, the Boomers see themselves as superior to others. They have always assumed that they could have life their way and that the rules were meant for others, but not for them. They feel entitled to rewards and view themselves as winners. They expect success and cannot accept failure.

Need for control: The Boomers need to feel certain and to sense that they are in control of life. They have a difficult time dealing with uncertainty.

Reflection: Baby Boomers have always valued introspection and take pleasure in asking questions.

For most people, life at age 45 or 50 doesn't match the dreams they had at age 20 or 30. When people reach age 45 or 50 and are even slightly disappointed by their achievements and experiences, their feelings are likely to be compounded by these factors of self-absorption, sense of entitlement, and a need for control. But there is also a positive side to this. The tendency to reflect and explore can help one look for new possibilities instead of being stuck with feelings of disappointment.

Keep all of this in mind as you complete the Midlife Checkup. It is a list of 29 unfinished sentences that will help you assess your life to date. The items on this list provide a framework for conducting your own assessment. Please add your own ideas that you think will help you reflect on your life's direction.

> **Please pass this newsletter along to a friend. Or call 555-0987 to request additional copies.**

The Midlife Checkup

1. My most important accomplish-ments are . . .

2. I am disappointed about . . .

3. I would describe the person I turned out to be as . . .

4. I want to change the following things about my self and my life . . .

5. Things I want to do before I die . . .

6. If I knew I couldn't fail, I would . . .

7. Things I have mastered . . .

8. Things I want to keep . . .

9. I want to keep these relationships . . .

10. I want to let go of these relationships . . .

11. I want to keep these possessions . . .

12. I want to let go of these possessions . . .

13. I want to have these experiences . . .

14. I want to clean up these messes . . .

15. I want to celebrate . . .

16. I don't ever again want to . . .

17. My body is . . .

18. My children are . . .

19. My parents are . . .

20. My spouse is . . .

21. I want to remember . . .

22. I want to forget . . .

23. I must apologize to . . .

24. I must seek an apology from . . .

25. I am most proud of . . .

26. I wish I could forget about . . .

27. I wish I could do over . . .

28. I wish I had never . . .

29. I wish I had . . .

30. Add your own items:

_____

_____

_____

_____

_____

Arnie Graham is a licensed counselor in Coral Gardens. He specializes in working with adolescents and their families. Call 555-0987 for your free consultation.

Life News

12. Simplify Your Life

By Elizabeth Handley, MSW

Most people say they want to simplify their lives because they feel like they have lost control of their time. They want to have more time to do the things they want to do, both at work and at home. Every few weeks, there is another newspaper or magazine story about how people feel that they aren't spending their time on things they enjoy. A recent poll, for example, found that 65% of people are spending their free time doing things they'd rather not do. Isn't that amazing? It's great if you have created a full and interesting life for yourself, but how frustrating if you don't have the time to enjoy it!

The 80/20 Principle

The 80/20 Principle, first stated by Vilfredo Pareto in 1897, says that 20% of our effort produces 80% of the results. This means that a small number of resources are highly productive—and a large number (80%) are not very productive at all. Here are a few examples:

- 20% of the things in your house are used 80% of the time.
- 80% of the things in your house are used 20% of the time.
- 20% of your activities give you 80% of your satisfaction.

- 20% of the stocks in an investor's portfolio produce 80% of the results.
- 20% of the books in a bookstore account for 80% of the sales.

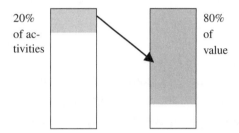

The challenge is to identify those few *vital* items that produce the greatest value for you. Focus on the activities that result in satisfaction, such as money, better health, or more free time. At the same time, identify those many *trivial* items that *don't* lead to things like satisfaction, money, better health, or more free time. These unprofitable activities are taking up 80% of your time. Doesn't it make sense to deemphasize them in favor of the vital 20%?

Making Time Takes Time

The first challenge to simplifying your life is that it takes an investment of time. If you want to discover how to make time for the things you enjoy, you have to examine how you are spending your time now. If you keep living your life the same way you always have, it will *stay* complicated.

For some, the excuse, "I can't slow down because everything is important," is a way to avoid seeing what they don't want to see: a relationship that is no longer fulfilling, a job that no longer satisfies, an emotional distance that has emerged between them and their family members. Some people keep their lives going at a furious pace to avoid seeing what they don't want to see.

If you really do want to simplify your life, you will make the time. You don't have to do anything radical; in fact, it is best to start small. Set aside just 30 minutes each day for a month. During that time, think about a simple question: What are the elements that contribute to my life feeling so complicated? Make a list of the factors in your private journal and write about them. Begin to think about what can be changed or eliminated.

Finding this time is not as impossible as it may seem at first. Maybe you can leave work 30 minutes early for a month and use the extra time for this exploration, possibly at home. Perhaps you can take the train instead of driving, or give up your exercise time for one month, or turn off the television during the evening news and write in your journal instead. Set aside 30 minutes a day for one month, ask yourself some important questions, and be prepared to learn some remarkable things about yourself.

Fewer Responsibilities

You may think that this sounds too simple. Most people who seek to simplify their lives think that the answer is to get more help. But this probably won't help. In fact, if you hire someone to help you get more done, you will actually have added another complication to your life rather than making it simpler. You

probably don't need more help; you probably need fewer responsibilities.

Learn to Say *No*

If you want a simpler life, you must learn to say *no*. In *Simplify Your Life: 100 Ways to Slow Down and Enjoy the Things That Really Matter,* author Elaine St. James says that people get into trouble because they agree to do things they really don't have time to do. This leads to a constant state of being overcommitted and frustrated. Our culture makes it difficult for us to say no to requests to attend extra meetings, dinner engagements, or to take on new responsibilities. Many of us feel obligated to always be participating at a high level. We are proud of our high productivity and involvement, but it comes with a high price: a complicated life that leaves to time for you. St. James suggests that you actually schedule time *for yourself* on your calendar at the beginning of every month; when you are invited to participate in something, turn down the request because you already have a commitment.

Clear Away Clutter

Get rid of things you don't use. Think of all the stuff you have acquired in the past five or 10 years. Most of it is designed to make life simpler, but in fact most of it brings along its own set of complications. Think of what typically happens when you buy a new electronic gadget: Consider all of the time required to earn the money to pay for it, shop for it, buy it, set it up, learn how to use it, fix the unexpected problems it causes with another gadget, and then the time you spend actually using it. Most of us have rooms in our houses filled with stuff that seemed like a good idea at the time, but ends up sitting on a shelf or in a drawer, unused. St. James suggests that you go through your house once each year and get rid of everything you haven't used during the previous year.

She also has an idea for not acquiring new stuff in the first place. She suggests a technique called the 30-Day List. When you start thinking that you must have a certain product, add it to your 30-Day List and wait. At the end of 30 days, ask yourself if you really still need it. Chances are, you will have lost your enthusiasm for the product and will cross it off the list.

Please pass this newsletter along to a friend. Or call 555-0987 to request additional copies.

Suggested Reading

Richard Koch, *The 80/20 Principle: The Secret of Achieving More With Less.* New York, NY: Doubleday, 1998.

Elaine St. James, *Simplify Your Life: 100 Ways to Slow Down and Enjoy the Things That Really Matter.* New York, NY: Hyperion, 1994.

Elizabeth Handley is a licensed social worker in Dana Point. She specializes in working with families and couples. Call 555-0987 for your free consultation.

The Good Life

13. Keeping Anger under Control

By Sharon Beck, M.A.

 In my work with individuals and couples, I see many people who have a difficult time expressing and managing angry feelings. Let's take a look at what causes people to become angry and how they can respond to stressful situations more productively.

What Is Anger?

Many people think that anger is caused by hormonal changes or brain activity. This is only partly true. Researchers have found that while hormones play a role in an angry response, there is always a cognitive (thinking) component.

Some people think that humans are innately aggressive or warlike. While our behavior is sometimes hostile toward others, anger is *not* part of our basic nature.

Frustration may lead to aggression, but it is *not* inevitable. Some people respond to frustrating events with anger, while others don't. Anger is only one response to frustration. In many cultures, people are taught to respond to frustration in other ways.

Since Freud's day, psychologists have disagreed about the value of venting feelings. It may surprise you to know that today's research shows that expressing anger often results in more irritation and tension rather than feeling more calm.

Why Expressing Anger Can Be Bad for You

Giving vent to anger can produce the following kinds of harmful effects:

- Your blood pressure increases.
- The original problem is worse rather than better.
- You come across as unfriendly and intimidating.
- The other person becomes angry with you as a result of your behavior.

Physical Effects of Anger

Heart. Researchers at Stanford University have found that of all the personality traits found in Type A patients, the potential for hostility is the key predictor for coronary disease. The combination of anger and hostility is the most deadly.

Stomach and intestines. Anger has a very negative effect on the stomach and has even been associated with the development of ulcerative colitis.

Nervous system. Anger is bad for you because it exaggerates the associated hormonal changes. Chronic suppressed anger is damaging because it activates the sympathetic nervous system responses without providing any release of the tension. It is a bit like stepping down on a car's accelerator while slamming on the brakes.

Why We Get into the Anger Habit

Anger is our response to stress. Many times we feel anger to avoid feeling some other emotion, such as anxiety or hurt. Or we may feel angry when we are frustrated because we want something and can't have it. Sometimes, feeling angry is a way of mobilizing ourselves in the face of a threat.

Anger may be useful because it stops (blocks) stress. Here are two examples:

1. You are rushing all day in your home office to meet an impossible deadline. Your daughter bounces in after school and gives you a big hug as you furiously type on your computer. You snap, "Not now! Can't you see I'm busy?"

2. You have just finished taking an important exam. You have studied for weeks and the result is very important to your career. You fantasize all the way home about dinner at your favorite Italian restaurant. When you get home, your husband has prepared a steak dinner for you. You yell, "Why don't you ask me before you just assume you know what I want?"

This explains why people often respond with anger when they experience the following kinds of stress:

- Anxiety
- Being in a hurry
- Being overstimulated
- Being overworked
- Depression
- Fatigue
- Fear
- Feeling abandoned or attacked
- Feeling forced to do something you don't want to do
- Feeling out of control
- Guilt, shame, or hurt
- Loss
- Physical pain

What to Do Instead of Getting Angry

Here are some constructive things can you do to reduce stress—instead of becoming angry:

- Beat a pillow with a tennis racket.
- Cry.
- Do relaxation exercises.
- Get physical exercise.
- Listen to your favorite music.
- Make a joke.
- Play games.
- Say it out loud.
- State your needs assertively.
- Take a nap.
- Tell a friend about it.
- Work.
- Write about it.

> **Please pass this newsletter along to a friend. Or call 555-0987 to request additional copies.**

New Responses to Stress

An angry response often results when we are unhappy with someone else's behavior. Here are some other responses you can choose instead of flying off the handle:

1. **Set limits.** Let's say a friend hasn't returned a book you loaned to her. Now she wants to borrow another one. You could say, "I'm not going to be able to lend you this book until you return the first one."
2. **Don't wait.** When you realize that you're feeling annoyed by a situation, speak up. Don't wait until your annoyance escalates to anger.
3. **Be assertive.** Say in a positive way what you want from the other person. For example, say, "Please call me when you get home," rather than, "Would you mind giving me a call when you get there?"

4 Ways to Stop the Spiral of Anger

1. **Call a time-out.** This is a very effective technique for breaking the sequence of behavior that leads to a blowup. It works best if it is discussed ahead of time and both people agree to use it. Here's how it works: Either person in an interaction can initiate time-out. One person makes the time-out gesture like a referee in a football game. The other person is obligated to return the gesture and stop talking.
2. **Check it out.** If anger is a response to personal pain, it makes sense to ask the other person, "What's hurting?"
3. **Make positive statements.** It may be helpful to memorize a few positive statements to say to yourself when your anger is being triggered. These statements can remind you that you can *choose* your behavior instead of reacting

in a knee-jerk manner—for example, "I can take care of my own needs," "His needs are just as important as mine," and "I am able to make good choices."
4. **Be prepared with a memorized response.** Here are a few statements and questions which will help deescalate anger:
   - What's bothering me is . . .
   - If it continues like this, I'll have to to take care of myself.
   - What do you need now?
   - So what you want is . . .

Suggested Reading

Matthew McKay, Peter Rogers, and Judith McKay, *When Anger Hurts: Quieting the Storm Within.* Oakland, CA: New Harbinger Publications, 1989.

Gayle Rosellini and Mark Worden, *Of Course You're Angry* (Second Edition). Center City, MN: Hazelden Foundation, 1997.

Carol Tavris, *Anger: The Misunderstood Emotion.* New York: Touchstone, 1989.

Sharon Beck, M.A. is a licensed counselor in Sierra Madre. She specializes in working with adolescents and their parents. Call 555-0987 for your free consultation.

14. Letting Go of the Past

By Juanita Perez, Ph.D.

People have a difficult time letting go of the past because they are held back by unfinished business. They may regret choices they have made or feel guilty about past actions. As long as guilt and regret are not resolved, it is difficult to move forward.

The Regret Epidemic

Regret is an emotion that feels similar to depression or sadness. It also feels like guilt, but it isn't the same thing. Sometimes a wave of regret seems to come out of nowhere. You might become aware of it when you lose something or someone, or when you meet someone from your past. It is a common feeling in our culture for several reasons.

1. **We have too many choices.** Since we have so many options, there are many more opportunities to regret the paths we *didn't* take.

    Example: When Linda was a senior at a major university, she interviewed with over 30 companies on campus. She was offered jobs in five different cities and had a difficult time choosing. In the end, she moved to Los Angeles and began an executive training program in a large company. A few years later, she began to wonder whether she had made the wrong choice. She thought she might have been better off in Kansas City, which had been her second choice. The regret leaves her feeling stuck and dissatisfied.

2. **Endless possibilities.** Another factor causing many of us to feel regret is that in the American culture, there is a belief that life has no limits. Our culture has an insatiable appetite for new experiences, adventure, and newness. When faced with the reality that certain things will not work out or change, we find it hard to accept.

    Example: Karen has turned 45. She has never married and has no children. She has always believed that "There is always tomorrow" and "I have plenty of time to make my mark." But now, realizing that she may never be a mother and probably won't be the CEO of her company, she is feeling like life has passed her by.

3. **No rules.** Along with all of these options, our lives have become confusing because there are few guidelines for what choices we should make.

    Example: Most women who have children struggle with the choices of what role employment should play in their lives, and many women feel like they made the wrong choice. Options include staying home with the children, working full-time at a demanding profession, or choosing a less demanding or part-time job.

Example: Many people feel compelled to continue on the ladder of success as long as they are being rewarded for it. When work becomes demanding and is no longer fun, it is hard to turn down promotions and pay increases in favor of less demanding, more satisfying work. People feel locked in to their career tracks and don't know how to get off the treadmill.

4. **We value self-sufficiency.** Our American culture has always valued independence. Somehow, we all get the message that it is better if we achieve our goals on our own, without the help of anyone else. The problem is that when we cannot accept support from others, we become isolated. Living a completely self-sufficient life violates the basic human need for affiliation.

Example: Matt's mother, Sarah, is 75. She is a widow and lives alone in an apartment in New York City. Matt left New York after finishing college and now lives in Florida. Sarah's friends are gradually moving to Florida, too. Matt has urged Sarah to move to a nearby condominium, and has even taken her to see a few of them. She resists, saying that she doesn't want to be a burden.

Meanwhile, Sarah is becoming increasingly isolated and depressed. She sits in her New York apartment and remembers the sunny condo she saw in Miami a few years back. She is filled with regret but won't change her mind. She feels like she has no choice but to remain independent and self-sufficient.

5. **Instant gratification.** Many people escape the pressures of daily life through drugs and alcohol. There are messages everywhere suggesting that we use alcohol and drugs to relax, escape, have fun, and be sexy. When this becomes a lifestyle, it often results in consequences that one can only regret: drunk driving, accidents, death and injury, relationship problems, poor attendance at work, or being fired.

6. **Constant comparisons.** When we compare our lives with others, it's easy to feel regret. Most of us expect ourselves to have it all together. We learn to act as if we are in control and compare ourselves with our friends, coworkers, neighbors, and the characters on television. When we don't look as good as they do, we feel like failures. We have a list of "shoulds" inside our heads—things we expect ourselves to be able to do.

Guilt

Guilt is usually the result of aggressive acts, wishes, and thoughts. It usually results from violating a rule—either our own or someone else's.

What to Do about Unfinished Business

If you want to move past the things in the past that are keeping you stuck—your unfinished business—you will need to acknowledge them and tell the truth about them. You don't necessarily have to take any action; sometimes just writing or talking about it is enough to lessen its impact. You can write about it in a private journal or talk about it with a trusted friend or counselor. Here are some places to look for your unfinished business:

1. Risks I should have taken

2. People I treated badly

3. People who treated me badly

4. Something I did to someone

5. Not doing something I should have done

6. Messes I need to clean up (literally and metaphorically)

7. Things I should throw away

8. Things I want to buy for my home

9. Things I want to buy for myself

10. Things I need but haven't allowed myself to have

11. Projects I've started but have not finished

12. Projects I want to start

13. Things I want to change

14. Things I want to stop doing

15. Things I want to be

16. Things I want to have

17. Experiences I want to have

18. Things I want to say

19. Feelings I have not expressed

20. Secrets I don't want to keep any longer

Suggested Reading

Carole Klein and Richard Gotti, *Overcoming Regret: Lessons from the Road Not Taken.* New York, Bantam Books, 1992.

Juanita Perez is a licensed psychologist in Arizona Springs. She specializes in helping people recover from addictions. Call 555-0987 for your free consultation.

Mental Health Express

15. Caring for the Caregiver

By Dolores Coburn, MSW

Few people are prepared for the responsibilities and tasks involved in caring for loved ones who are ill, elderly, or disabled. The success of the relationship between you and your loved one depends on several factors. One of the most important is how well you take care of yourself, empowering yourself to be there for the person you are caring for. Let's look first at what causes the stress in such a relationship, and then we will explore some ways to care for yourself as you care for another.

Sources of Stress

Caring for someone who is sick or disabled causes tremendous stress. This stress comes from several directions and each has a different effect on the caregiver. The following are the main sources of such stress:

1. **Being far away:** In most families, people are spread out across the country and are not always available to help with caring for a sick or elderly person. This places extra stress on the person nearby, who often must contribute the most in terms of time and money toward the patient's care. The out-of-towners may not realize how much time and money the person close at hand is devoting to the care of their family member.

2. **Financial stress** is inevitable when someone requires an excessive amount of care. For example:

   a. Many caregivers spend their own money to cover expenses that are not covered by insurance or Medicare.

   b. The family members who are less involved may not realize how expensive certain items are and may even resist helping to pay for them.

   c. The primary caregiver may have to work fewer hours or find less demanding work (which may pay less money). Many caregivers have to stop working completely in order to care for the patient.

3. **Cultural expectations:** In some cultures, daughters are expected to care for parents, and in others it is not acceptable to place relatives in nursing homes.

4. **Relationship stress:** In addition to the financial stress, all of these factors create enormous stress on the relationships among family members. This can lead to an additional layer of problems if it is not openly discussed and resolved.

5. **Physical stress:** Caring for an ailing person can be a physical challenge. Activities like cooking, cleaning, doing

laundry, and shopping can be exhausting, especially when they are added to the responsibilities of your own life.

6. **Home alterations:** If the patient continues to live at home, you may need to make alterations such as building ramps or railings. Everyone in the home will have to adjust.

7. **Social stress:** Providing personal care 24 hours a day can cut off the primary caregiver from family and friends. You may be too tired to have an evening out, or you may not have anyone else to take over. This can result in your feeling angry and resentful toward the person you are caring for.

8. **Emotional stress:** As a result of these stresses, it is not unusual to feel a range of emotions, including anger, resentment, anxiety, frustration, sadness, and guilt. These negative emotions may conflict with the love you feel for your family member and the satisfaction you feel from contributing to the quality of his or her life.

With all of these kinds of stress, it is not surprising that many caregivers become overwhelmed and begin to feel burned out.

Signs That a Caregiver Needs Help

How do you know if the stress is becoming too much for you? The following is a list of signs that you need help. Take a moment to look through these and identify those that are now problems for you or may be potential problems.

1. You don't get out much anymore.
2. You argue with the person you care for.
3. You have conflicts with other family members.
4. You abuse drugs, alcohol, or medications.
5. Your appetite has changed.
6. You isolate yourself from others.
7. You behave in a compulsive manner or are overly focused on minor details.
8. You feel listless; you lack energy.
9. You feel more angry, anxious, or worried than usual.
10. You have a difficult time controlling your emotions.
11. You have a hard time concentrating.
12. You have physical symptoms of anxiety, such as an upset stomach, headaches, or a racing heart.
13. You often forget things.
14. You are clumsy or accident-prone.
15. You have self-destructive or suicidal thoughts.
16. You sleep more or less than usual.
17. You never seem to get enough rest.
18. You feel guilty about your situation.

Caregiver Survival Tips

1. Find out about resources before you need them. For example, don't delay researching nursing homes until the patient needs to be placed in one.
2. Seek all the support you can find. Be on the lookout for groups, individuals, and

organizations that provide emotional, social, physical, and financial support.

3. Ask your family and friends for help. They may be able to provide you with time, knowledge, or money.

4. Investigate adult day care facilities. They offer therapeutic, rehabilitative, and support services such as nursing, social work services, meals, or transportation.

5. Consider having meals delivered. Many organizations provide nutritional programs.

6. Consider hiring a home health aide. Aides can provide personal care at home such as help with eating, dressing, oral hygiene, bathing, administering medication, and light household tasks.

7. Find out about homemaker services. These services can assist with shopping, laundry, housecleaning, preparing meals, and taking clients to medical appointments.

8. Look into the offerings of hospital and surgical supply services. They rent or sell medical supplies and equipment like hospital beds, canes, walkers, bath chairs, oxygen, and other equipment.

9. Check out respite care services. They provide relief to caregivers.

10. Look into social day care. They provide recreational activities, social work services, hot meals, transportation, and some health services.

11. Find out about transportation services. They provide transportation to and from medical appointments or other care services.

12. Find out about skilled nursing services. They offer professional help with specific medical problems.

13. Maintain your interests. Keep balance in your life.

14. Be realistic about what you can accomplish. Recognize what you can and cannot do.

15. Maintain communication with your family and friends. When tensions and misunderstandings develop (and they will), address them quickly.

16. Take care of yourself. Eat well, exercise, rest, and take time off.

Suggested Reading

Claire Berman, *Caring for Yourself While Caring for Your Aging Parents: How to Help, How to Survive*. New York, NY: Henry Holt and Co., 1996.

Cathy Booth, Taking Care of Our Aging Parents. *Time* Magazine, August 30, 1999.

Avrene Brandt, *Caregiver's Reprieve: A Guide to Emotional Survival when You're Caring for Someone You Love*. San Luis Obispo, CA: Impact Publishers, 1998.

John Greenwald, Elder Care: Making the Right Choice. *Time* Magazine, August 30, 1999.

David Haigler, Kathryn Mims, and Jack Nottingham, *Caring for You, Caring for Me: Education and Support for Caregivers*. Americus, GA: Rosalynn Carter Institute at Georgia Southwestern State University, 1998.

Billie Jackson, *The Caregivers' Roller Coaster: A Practical Guide to Caregiving for the Frail Elderly*. Chicago, IL: Loyola University Press, 1993.

Dolores Coburn is a licensed Clinical Social Worker in Woodstock. She specializes in stress management and biofeedback. Call 555-0987 for your free consultation.

Feeling Good

16. Moving beyond Grief and Loss

By Sam Patterson, MSW

In my work as a mental health professional, I have seen many clients dealing with losses of all kinds—loss of loved ones through death and divorce, for instance. These experiences are difficult for everyone.

Stages of Recovery from Loss

There are some predictable stages that most people pass through after losing something or someone important. In her work on death and dying, Elisabeth Kübler-Ross outlined five stages of grieving.

Shock and Denial: The first reaction to loss is often the inability to feel anything. This may include feeling numb, weak, overwhelmed, anxious, not yourself, or withdrawn.

Anger: Blaming yourself or others for the loss.

Bargaining: "If you'll just let him live, I'll promise to go to church every Sunday for the rest of my life."

Depression: Feeling deep sadness, disturbed sleep and eating patterns, thoughts of suicide, excessive crying.

Acceptance: Beginning to look for the lessons of the experience.

Kübler-Ross said that the grieving process involves experiencing all five stages, although not always in this order. She also said that people often cycle back and forth through a number of the stages before coming to the stage of acceptance.

Kinds of Losses

Some examples of significant losses are:

- Loss of a person through death
- Divorce
- Job loss
- Loss of your good health when you are diagnosed with a disease
- Loss of a body part through accident or surgery
- Loss of an ability, such as blindness
- Loss of a friend who has moved
- Loss of everything familiar when you move away

Each kind of loss affects each person in a different way, but the recovery process usually follows Kübler-Ross's five stages.

Recovering from Loss:
Some Key Points

1. **You are responsible for your own grief process.** No one can tell you how to grieve, and no one will do your grieving for you. It is hard work and you must manage the process by yourself.

2. **The grief process has a purpose.** It is to help you learn to accept the reality of the loss and to learn from the experience.

3. **Remind yourself that your grief will end.** You will not feel like this forever. You will heal.

4. **Take care of your health.** Grief is extremely stressful, and it requires energy to manage the stress.

5. **Be careful with food and drink.** While it may be tempting to numb the pain with food and drink, this can lead to the additional problems of alcohol dependence and overweight. Also, numbing the pain means you are prolonging denial. This will make your grieving process longer.

6. **Talk about the person** who is no longer in your life. People sometimes avoid talking about the loss as a denial mechanism. However, this prolongs denial and the grieving process.

7. **Take time to be alone.** In the days and weeks following the loss of a loved one, there is often a flurry of activity with many visitors and phone calls. Added to

> **Don't make any important decisions until your life feels more balanced. It can be tempting to make some important changes right after a major loss as an effort to feel more in control.**

the stress of your loss, this can be completely exhausting. People will understand if you don't answer the phone for an afternoon or go to your room and close the door for a while.

8. **Maintain a normal routine if you can.** You have enough changes in your life right now. Try to get up in the morning, go to bed at night, and take your meals at the same times you usually do.

9. **Ask for help.** You will need it. If you don't want to be alone, or if you want someone to take you somewhere, it is okay to ask. People don't expect you to be self-sufficient right now.

10. **Let people help you.** People want to help because it gives them a way to express their feelings. Staying connected with people is especially important now, and accepting help is a way of staying connected.

11. **Keep a journal of your feelings and experiences** during the grief process. Writing about your feelings helps you express them, rather than keeping them inside. It also gives you something to remember and review in the future, which you will appreciate.

> **Writing about your feelings helps you express them, rather than keeping them inside.**

12. **Avoid making extreme life changes** after a major loss. Don't make any important decisions until your life feels more balanced. It can be tempting to make some important changes right after a major loss as an effort to feel more in control. If you can, put off such changes and decisions until later.

13. **Don't hurry your grief process.** People sometimes want to put their feelings and memories behind them because they are painful. But grieving takes time, and there are no shortcuts.
14. **Remind yourself** that although grief hurts, it will not harm you. Grief is painful, but you will survive and even grow from the experience.
15. **Expect to regress** in your recovery process from time to time. This is normal. It may happen unexpectedly, but it probably won't last long.
16. **Acknowledge the anniversary** of your loss by taking the day off or doing something special. Have supportive people ready to be with you. It could be a difficult day and it's better not to be alone.

How to Help Someone Who Is Grieving

1. Don't try to get them to feel or be anything but what they are.
2. Don't reward them for acting cheerful or "like your old self." This teaches them to suppress their feelings around you.
3. Don't avoid them. They need your support.
4. Let them tell about the loss again and again, if they need to.
5. Recognize that unexpected, perhaps inappropriate behavior is part of the grieving process. It means the bereaved person is moving forward.

Suggested Reading

Bob Deits, *Life After Loss.* Tucson, AZ: Fisher Books, 1992.

Elisabeth Kubler-Ross, *On Death and Dying.* New York: MacMillan: 1969.

Sam Patterson, MSW is a licensed Social Worker in Springfield. He specializes in the issues of grief and loss and works with individuals, couples and families. Call 555-4567 to request additional copies of this newsletter or to schedule a free consultation.

The Maple Leaf Express

17. Managing Perfectionism

By Krystal DeVries, M.A.

What Is Perfectionism?

This is the first of two newsletters that address perfectionism. In this issue, we will explore what perfectionism is and why it is destructive. In the next one, we will take a look at some strategies for both controlling the need to be perfect and living a more relaxed, satisfying life.

Perfectionists aspire to be top achievers and do not allow themselves to make even a single mistake. They are always on the alert for imperfections and weaknesses in themselves and others. They tend to be rigid thinkers who are on the lookout for deviations from the rules or the norm.

Perfectionism is not the same as striving for excellence. People who pursue excellence in a healthy way take genuine pleasure in working to meet high standards. Perfectionists are motivated by self-doubt and fears of disapproval, ridicule, and rejection. The high producer *has drive,* while the perfectionist *is driven.*

Causes and Characteristics

Fear of failure and rejection. The perfectionist believes that she will be rejected or fail if she is not always perfect, so she becomes paralyzed and unable to produce or perform at all.

Fear of success. The perfectionist believes that if he is successful in what he undertakes, he will have to keep it up. This becomes a heavy burden—who wants to operate at such a high level all of the time?

Low self-esteem. A perfectionist's needs for love and approval tend to blind her to the needs and wishes of others. This makes it difficult or impossible to have healthy relationships with others.

Black-and-white thinking. Perfectionists see most experiences as either good or bad, perfect or imperfect. There is nothing in between. The perfectionist believes that the flawless product or superb performance must be produced every time. Perfectionists believe if it can't be done perfectly, it's not worth doing.

Extreme determination. Perfectionists are determined to overcome all obstacles to achieving success. This is also true of high achievers, but the perfectionist focuses only on the *result* of his efforts. He is unable to enjoy the *process* of producing the achievement. His relentless pursuit of the goal becomes his downfall because it often results in overwhelming anxiety, sabotaging his heroic efforts.

The Costs of Being a Perfectionist

Perfectionism always costs more than the benefits it might provide. It can result in being paralyzed with fear and becoming so rigid that a person is difficult to relate to. It can produce contradictory styles, from being highly productive to being completely nonproductive. Some examples of these costs include the following:

Low self-esteem. Just as low self-esteem is a cause of perfectionist behavior, it is also a result. Because a perfectionist never feels good enough about himself or his personal performance, he usually feels like a loser or a failure.

Gloominess. Since a perfectionist is convinced that it will be next to impossible to achieve most goals, she can easily develop a negative attitude.

Depression. Perfectionists often feel discouraged and depressed because they are driven to be perfect but know that it is impossible to reach the ideal.

Guilt. Perfectionists never think they handle things well. They often feel a sense of shame and guilt as a result.

Rigidity. Since perfectionists need to have everything meet an ideal, they tend to become inflexible and lack spontaneity.

Lack of motivation. A person who expects perfection may never try new behaviors or learn new skills because she thinks that she will never be able to do it well enough. At other times, she may begin the new behavior but give up early because she fears that she will never reach her goal.

Paralysis. Since most perfectionists have an intense fear of failure, they sometimes become immobilized and stagnant. Writers who suffer from writer's block are examples of the perfectionist's paralysis.

Obsessive behavior. When a person needs a certain order or structure in his life, he may become overly focused on details and rules.

Compulsive behavior. A perfectionist who feels like a failure or loser may medicate him- or herself with alcohol, drugs, food, shopping, sex, gambling, or other high-risk behaviors.

Eating disorders. Many studies have determined that perfectionism is a central issue for people who develop eating disorders.

The Perfectionist versus The High Achiever

People produce many of their best achievements when they are striving to do their best. High achievers, like perfectionists, want to be better people and achieve great things. Unlike perfectionists, high achievers accept that making mistakes and risking failure are part of the achievement process—and part of being human.

Emotionally Healthy High Producers

You can be a high achiever without being a perfectionist. People who accomplish plenty and stay emotionally healthy tend to exhibit the following behaviors:

- Set standards that are high but achievable.
- Enjoy the process, not just the outcome.
- Recover from disappointment quickly.
- Are not disabled by anxiety and fear of failure.
- View mistakes as opportunities for growth and learning.
- React positively to constructive feedback.

Once you are aware of the ways by which you expect yourself to be perfect, you can start to change your behavior. In my next newsletter, I'll offer some tips to help you get started. Until then, begin the change process by thinking about which causes apply to you and writing down examples of these perfectionist behaviors as you observe them.

_____

Krystal DeVries is a licensed staff counselor at the Maple Center in Westbrook. Call 555-0987 for your free consultation.

The Extraordinary Life

18. How to Be Less of a Perfectionist and Enjoy Life More

By Pat James, M.A.

This is the second of a series of two newsletters that explore the dynamics of perfectionism. In my last newsletter, you learned what perfectionism is and why people develop the need to do things perfectly. In this issue, you will learn how to change your perfectionist behaviors and enable yourself to be more satisfied with yourself and your life.

You will have the greatest success if you read the first newsletter and take some time to observe your own perfectionist patterns. Once you have accomplished that, choose a few of the strategies outlined here. Keep working at it until you understand what you need to do to accept your imperfections and humanness.

Create a Support Network for Yourself

Seek out people who are not perfectionists. Encourage your support network to not be rigid or moralistic in their attempts to keep you on an honest course. Look for people who forgive and forget when mistakes, failures, offenses, or backsliding occur. Ask them to tell you when they think you are being rigid, unrealistic, or idealistic in your behavior. Ask them to give you positive reinforcement for any positive change, no matter how small. Seek out people who have a sincere interest in your personal growth.

Do Some Self-Exploration

Explore the following questions in your journal, make some notes here, or discuss them with a trusted friend or professional counselor:

1. Where do you see perfectionist behavior in your life?

   _____
   _____
   _____
   _____

2. How do these behaviors create problems for you?

   _____
   _____
   _____
   _____

3. What perfectionist beliefs do you have?
_____
_____
_____
_____

4. How do you think these beliefs will affect your ability to change your behavior?
_____
_____
_____
_____

5. What do you need to do to become less of a perfectionist and more relaxed about things?
_____
_____
_____
_____

6. How can you use your support system to help yourself be less of a perfectionist?
_____
_____
_____
_____

Note your own examples here: _____
_____
_____
_____

Perfectionist behaviors: _____
_____
_____
_____

Alternative behaviors: _____
_____
_____
_____

Lower Your Expectations

It is very important to understand that it is unrealistic to expect to change your behavior (or someone else's) immediately or completely.

Identify Alternative Behaviors

Make a list of specific perfectionist behaviors that you want to change. For each one, think of something specific you could do instead. For example:

- *Perfectionist behavior:* I expect my teenage daughter to pick up the clothes off her floor and make her bed every day.
- *Alternative behavior:* I can expect my daughter to clean her room every Saturday and I will close her door every other day.

Make a List of the Advantages and Disadvantages of Being Perfect

You may find that perfection is too costly. Perhaps you will discover that relationship problems, endless working, and other compulsive behaviors (eating disorders and substance abuse problems) are too high a price for the results you gain from your perfectionist way of being.

Pay Attention to Your Behavior and Attitudes

As you see yourself behaving in a perfectionist way, take note. In the beginning, just observe yourself. Keep a log if it helps you see your behavior more clearly. You don't have to make any changes until you have a good idea of your specific behaviors and thoughts.

Try Some New Thoughts and Behaviors

Begin to substitute the alternative behaviors you identified earlier. If possible, ask someone from your support network for feedback. Observe your feelings and thoughts as you try new things.

Review Your Goals and Make Sure They Are Realistic

By having achievable, realistic goals, you will gradually see that less-than-perfect results are not as disastrous as you thought they would be.

Set Strict Time Limits for Your Projects

When the time is up, move on to another task or take a break.

Make Friends with Criticism

Many perfectionists take criticism personally and respond defensively. If someone criticizes you when you make a mistake, the easiest thing to do is to simply admit it. Remind yourself that you are human, meaning you will sometimes make mistakes. The people who never make mistakes are no longer learning or growing.

> **Learn to re-frame criticism and see it as information you can learn from.**

When you let go of the fantasy that humans must be perfect to have value in this world, you are less likely to feel angry or embarrassed when you make a mistake. You will see that criticism is information that you can learn from, and you will no longer need to avoid it.

> **Please pass this newsletter along to a friend. Or call 555-0987 to request additional copies.**

Pat James is Executive Director of the State & Main Therapy Center in Allendale. Call 555-0987 for your free consultation.

Mental Health Review

19. What Makes You Procrastinate?

By Cass Jameson, M.S.

The first in a series of two newsletters, this issue deals with why we procrastinate.

All of us procrastinate on occasion. For some people, it's a chronic problem; for others, it's only a problem in certain life areas. Procrastination is always frustrating because it results in wasted time, lost opportunities, disappointing work performance, and generally feeling bad about yourself.

When you procrastinate, you allow less important tasks to take up the time and space that should be devoted to more important things. You do things like hanging out with friends when you know that an important work project is due soon, or going shopping instead of doing your homework. It can also be evident in behavior such as talking about trivial things with your partner to avoid discussing important issues in your relationship.

Most people don't have a problem finding time for things they *want* to do. But once they see a task as too difficult, painful, boring, or overwhelming, the procrastination behaviors begin. You are not alone if you have ever made any of the following excuses to yourself:

1. It's too cold to exercise outside today. I'll wait until tomorrow when it's warmer.

2. I've got too many other things to do first.

3. I'll do a better job when I can concentrate on this project.

4. I still have lots of time to get this done.

5. They don't pay me enough to do a more complete job. This is good enough.

6. This problem is too hard to talk about. I wouldn't know where to start.

7. I work better under pressure.

8. It's too noisy to work while my teenager is at home.

9. I should get the shopping down now because the stores will be more crowded later.

10. I can eat this pie tonight, because I'm starting my diet tomorrow.

11. My tooth doesn't really hurt that much. The pain will probably go away tomorrow.

Most of the time, these excuses seem fairly innocuous. However, they're not as innocent as they seem, because they cause us to postpone important duties and projects. Ultimately, these excuses can keep us from accomplishing important goals and make us feel bad about ourselves.

Why People Procrastinate

If you were hoping for a simple answer to this puzzle, you will be disappointed to learn that there are many reasons why people put things off. Here are a few of the most common (check those that apply to you):

☐ **Avoiding discomfort.** Wanting to avoid pain makes lots of people shift into procrastination mode. However, the longer we delay, the worse the uncomfortable problem usually becomes. The rash gets bigger, the tooth hurts more, or the brakes squeak even more loudly.

☐ **Perfectionism.** Those who believe they must produce the perfect report may obsess about uncovering every last information source and then write draft after draft. Their search for the perfect product takes up so much time that they miss their deadline.

☐ **Laziness.** Sometimes people delay tasks that involve fairly slight inconvenience or minor discomfort.

☐ **Thinking you're not good enough.** Some people are certain that they are incompetent. They think that they will

---

Physics Review
Remember the concept of inertia: a mass at rest tends to *stay* at rest.

---

fail, and procrastinate to avoid ever putting their skills to the test.

☐ **Self-doubt.** If you second-guess yourself, you probably suffer from procrastination. You may avoid new challenges and opportunities unless you are certain that you will succeed. Perhaps you make feeble attempts to begin a project, and you tell yourself that you could do a better job if you put in more effort.

☐ **Workaholism.** At the other end of the spectrum, many people who work excessively also fall into this category. They drive themselves ruthlessly, fearing that if they stop working, they will not be able to start again. Most self-doubters are driven by the belief that they must meet strict standards in order to see themselves as successful.

For some reason, it is more difficult for most humans to *start* change than to *keep it going.*

Why Don't We Just Say *No?*

Since procrastination produces mostly negative outcomes, why don't we just change our behavior and eliminate these undesirable consequences? The reason for this is that *procrastination reinforces itself.* For some reason, it is more difficult for most humans to *start* change than to *keep it going.* We avoid getting started by cleverly diverting our attention from the things we really should be doing. We do something else instead or make up a story about how we will accomplish the

task in the future—when we are inspired, or when we have completed a preliminary step, or some other trick.

Although recognizing how these diversions work won't automatically cure your procrastination, being aware of it is a good place to start working on the problem. Once you are aware of the ways that *you* procrastinate, you can start to change your behavior. In my next newsletter, I'll offer some tips to help you get started. Until then, begin the change process by thinking about which causes apply to you and writing down examples of these behaviors as you observe them.

> **Please pass this newsletter along to a friend. Or call 555-0987 to request additional copies.**

Cass Jameson is a Licensed Counselor and Clinical Director of the Mountain Hills Center. Call 555-0987 for your free consultation.

Oak Center News

20. How to Stop Procrastinating

By Laurel Kaplan, Center Director

This is the second of a series of two newsletters that explore the dynamics of procrastination. In my last newsletter, you learned what procrastination is and why people do it. In this issue, you will learn how to change your procrastination behaviors and enable yourself to be more productive.

You will have the greatest success if you read the first newsletter and take some time to observe your own procrastination patterns. Once you have accomplished that, choose a few of the strategies outlined here. Keep working at it until you understand what you need to do to stop putting things off.

Set Specific Goals

The most effective goals are specific, measurable, and achievable. An example of a good goal is, "I will buy paint on Friday and paint the living room on Saturday." This is better than saying, "I am going to get the house ready to sell."

Set Priorities

Write down all the things that you need to do, and place them in order of importance. The most important tasks belong at the top of your list and the distractions go at the bottom. Start at the top of your list and work your way down.

Organize Your Work

Set up a system for yourself. Prepare a daily schedule and keep it within view during your working time. List the tasks for each day. Check things off as you complete them. When you are working on a project, lay out all of the needed supplies or materials before you begin.

Divide and Conquer

Sometimes a project is overwhelming if you think about all of the work that is involved. Do yourself a favor: Break the activity down into smaller steps and set progress goals for each of the steps. This is especially helpful when you are beginning a writing project, studying for a degree, or building a new set of skills.

For example, if you need to write a report, make an outline before you start writing. If you have to clean your house, make your goal to do the first two rooms by 10:00, two more by noon, and two more by 2:00. Check tasks off your outline as you complete them.

Make It a Game

Turn the temptation to avoid working into a challenge. Use your imagination. For example, if you need to study the first five chapters of your history book, pretend that you are a substitute teacher and will need to lecture on the material tomorrow. Take notes and organize the information into an outline that you could speak from. Sometimes changing the frame around a situation makes it more interesting and less of a chore.

Schedule a Small Amount of Time

Tell yourself that you will only spend ten minutes on the task right now, just to get your feet wet. Work on the task for the ten minutes and then choose whether to continue for ten *more* minutes. Continue doing this until you decide to stop, or when you are finished with the task. If you stop working on the task before it is finished, spend a few more minutes to plan a strategy for the next steps.

When you are tempted to substitute a fun but unimportant activity (such as reading a magazine or watching the weather channel) for an important project (such as finishing pages of your report), make the substitute activity your reward for doing the important task. Do the high-priority job first and reward yourself with the fun activity.

Ward Off Self-Defeating Thoughts

Telling yourself that you are going to do a poor job or even fail can seriously undermine your ability to function. It is important to realize that your negative statements are not facts. Keep your focus on the present moment and the positive steps you can take toward accomplishing your goals. If these thoughts are based on a need for perfection or low self-esteem (described in the "Managing Perfectionism" newsletter), you may want to work on these issues.

Make a Commitment

Make a verbal and written commitment to completing the task or project. Write a contract and sign it. Tell someone about your plans and ask them to follow up with you.

One trainer wanted to create a how-to workbook and market it to other training professionals. After weeks of procrastination, she decided to motivate herself by creating a deadline. She wrote an ad for the workbook and placed it in the professional publication that she knew her colleagues would be reading. When her telephone began to ring with orders for the workbook, she suddenly became very focused.

Remind Yourself

Write notes to yourself and post them in conspicuous places. Leave them where you will see them—on places like the outside of your briefcase, the bathroom mirror, refrigerator, television, your front door, and the dashboard of your car. The more often you remind yourself of what you plan to accomplish, the more likely it is that you will follow through with action.

Reward Yourself

Reinforcement is a very effective way to motivate yourself. When you complete even the most minor task, be sure to acknowledge what you have done. This is especially important in the beginning when you are struggling with procrastination behaviors. After you have mastered these issues and have regained your peak productivity, don't forget to celebrate the completion of the big projects. You worked hard for it and shouldn't take it for granted.

Use the information from this newsletter to develop your personal program for accomplishing the things that are most important to you.

How will you use this information to improve the quality of your life? Write your notes here:

_____

_____

_____

_____

_____

_____

_____

_____

_____

_____

_____

_____

_____

Laurel Kaplan is Clinical Director of the Oak Center in Georgetown. Call 555-0987 for your free consultation.

Chestnut Hill Monthly News

21. Recovering from Sexual Assault

By Stella Harrison, BSW

Sexual assault occurs when one person forces any unwanted sexual contact onto another person. It can involve a stranger, friend, partner, or acquaintance. It can involve any type of unwanted sexual behavior.

Being sexually assaulted involves both physical and psychological assault. Assault victims experience a range of emotions that include fear, shame, anger, and depression.

Most sexual assault victims are women, and most perpetrators are men. However, a significant number of males also are sexually assaulted. For the sake of simplicity, I will refer to the victims in this article as females.

Stages of Sexual Assault Recovery

Sexual assault victims usually have emotional and physical reactions that fall into three stages. These can be described as shock, adjustment, and resolution.

Shock usually lasts from a few hours to several weeks. The victim experiences shock, disbelief, fear, and anger. She may have phobic reactions to the place where the sexual assault occurred. She may also have flashbacks, an immediate sense of reliving the sexual assault, and trouble sleeping.

Adjustment comes next. During this temporary stage, the victim begins to feel like her life is returning to normal and tries to regain some sense of control. She may deny the impact of the assault.

Resolution is the time when healing occurs. It is often an uncomfortable period for the victim. She may have many of the same feelings that she experienced immediately following the assault, but now she is closer to being ready to resolve them. She may feel depressed, experience mood swings, feel cut off from others, or need to isolate herself. During this stage of recovery, many victims seek the services of a professional counselor.

Common Responses to Sexual Assault

Most sexual assault victims report some of the following physical and emotional symptoms:

Apathy
Difficulty concentrating
Eating disorders
Feeling nervous or jumpy
Feelings of depression, sadness, and hope-
    lessness
Guilt
Headaches
Hypervigilance
Inability to express emotions
Inability to trust others
Insomnia
Irritability and anger
Isolation
Less interest in activities
Less interest in sex
Loss of self-esteem
Nausea and vomiting
Nightmares and flashbacks
Panic attacks
Physical pain
Poor appetite
Post-Traumatic Stress Disorder (chronic anx-
    iety, depression, and flashbacks)
Self-mutilation
Shame and embarrassment
Shock and denial
Substance abuse
Thoughts of suicide and death

Recovery Steps

Crisis intervention is an important first step. The first few days after an assault can be especially turbulent, and victims need the unique skills of counselors who are trained to respond to crises.

Individual counseling is highly recommended. Any person who has been sexually assaulted will benefit from individual counseling sessions with a caring, experienced, mental health professional.

Group therapy for sexual assault victims is an excellent way for victims to talk about their experiences with others in a supportive and nonjudgmental atmosphere.

Couples counseling can help the victim and her partner to explore their feelings, talk about how the assault is impacting their relationship, and learn coping skills.

Recovery Prognosis

Since every person and situation is different, victims of sexual assault respond to an assault in different ways. Many factors can influence an individual's recovery from sexual assault. Some examples include the following:

- The circumstances surrounding the assault
- The severity of the assault
- The victim's relationship to the perpetrator
- How police and medical workers respond to the assault
- The victim's age and maturity level
- How the victim views the attack and what meaning she gives it
- The victim's support system

- The quality of the response of the victim's family and friends
- Community attitudes toward sexual assault

Based on these factors, some survivors of sexual assault recover fairly quickly. Others feel the effects of the experience throughout their lifetime.

Please pass this newsletter along to a friend. Or call 555-0987 to request additional copies.

Stella Harrison manages the Sexual Assault Recovery Program at Chestnut Hill Center. Call 555-0987 for your free consultation.

22. What to Do about the Holiday Blues

By Red Doran, ACSW

Not everyone shares in the celebration and joy associated with the holidays. Many people feel stressed and unhappy in response to the demands of shopping for gifts, spending large amounts of money, attending parties and family gatherings, and entertaining houseguests. It is not uncommon to react to these stresses with excessive drinking and eating, difficulty sleeping, and physical complaints. The holiday blues are a common result. If you experience reactions like these during the holidays, you are not alone. Let's take a look at what causes the holiday blues and what you can do about them.

What Causes the Holiday Blues?

Fear of disappointing others. Some people fear disappointing their loved ones during the holidays. Even though they can't afford to spend a lot of money on gifts, some people feel so obligated to come through with a fancy gift that they spend more than they can afford.

Expecting gifts to improve relationships. Giving someone a nice present won't necessarily strengthen a friendship or romantic relationship. When your gifts don't produce the reactions you had hoped for, you may feel let down.

Anniversary reactions. If someone important to you passed away or left you during a past holiday season, you may become depressed as the anniversary approaches.

Bad memories. For some families, the holidays are times of chaos and confusion. This is especially true in families where people have substance abuse problems or dysfunctional ways of relating to each other. If this was true in your family in past years, you may always carry memories of the disappointment and upheaval that came with the holidays. Even though things may be better now, it is difficult to forget the times when your holidays were ruined by substance abuse and family dysfunction.

It could be SAD. People who live in northern states may experience depression during the winter because of Seasonal Affective Disorder (SAD). SAD results from fewer hours of sunlight as the days grow shorter during the winter months.

Strategies for Dealing with the Holiday Blues

While the holiday blues are usually temporary, these ideas can help make this year's holiday experience more pleasant and less stressful.

Be realistic. Don't expect the holiday season to solve all past problems. The forced cheerfulness of the holiday season cannot ward off sadness or loneliness.

Drink less alcohol. Even though drinking alcohol gives you a temporary feeling of well-being, it is a depressant and never makes anything better.

Give yourself permission not to feel cheerful. Accept how you are feeling. If you have recently experienced a loss, you can't expect yourself to put on a happy face. Tell others how you are feeling and what you need.

Have a spending limit and stick to it. Look for holiday activities that are free, such as driving around to look at holiday decorations. Go window-shopping without purchasing anything. Look for ways to show people you care without spending a lot.

Be honest. Express your feelings to those around you in a constructive, honest, and open way. If you need to confront someone with a problem, begin your sentences with "I feel."

Look for sources of support. Learn about offerings at mental health centers, churches, and synagogues. Many of these have special support groups, workshops, and other activities designed to help people deal with the holiday blues.

Give yourself special care. Schedule times to relax and pamper yourself. Take a warm bath or spend an evening with a good book.

Set limits and priorities. Be realistic about what you will be able to accomplish. Prepare a To-Do list to help you arrange your priorities.

Volunteer your time. If you are troubled because you won't be seeing your family, volunteer to work at a hospital or food bank. Volunteering can help raise your spirits by turning your focus to people who are less fortunate than you are.

Get some exercise. Exercise has a positive impact on depression because it boosts serotonin levels. Try to get some type of exercise at least twice each week.

After the Holidays

For some people, holiday blues continue into the new year. This is often caused by leftover feelings of disappointment during the holiday season and being physically exhausted. The blues also happen for some people because

the start of a new year is a time of reflection, which can produce anxiety.

Is It More than Just the Holiday Blues?

Clinical depression is more than just feeling sad for a few weeks. The symptoms generally include changes in appetite and sleep patterns, having less interest in daily activities, difficulty concentrating, and a general feeling of hopelessness.

Clinical depression requires professional treatment. If you are concerned that a friend

or relative may be suffering from more than just holiday blues, you should express your concerns. If the person expresses thoughts of worthlessness or suicide, it is important to seek the help of a qualified mental health professional.

> **For further information, visit these web sites:**
>
> **American Psychological Association: www.apa.org**
>
> **National Depressive and Manic-Depressive Association: www.ndmda.org**
>
> **National Mental Health Association: www.nmha.org**

Red Doran is the Director of the Children's Therapy Center in DuPage Beach. Call 555-0987 for your free consultation.

Psych Update

23. What Causes All of This Stress?

By Bob West, Ph.D.

In this newsletter, we will explore what stress is and what causes it. In the next, you will learn how to manage the stress in your life and protect yourself against it.

Stress Is a Response

Most experts define stress as a response to life situations like the following:

1. Having too many responsibilities
2. Vague or confusing expectations
3. Having to do unpleasant tasks
4. Facing too many distractions
5. Having to do tasks for which one is unprepared
6. Working with difficult people
7. Being bored
8. Being sick
9. Experiencing too many changes
10. Being in physical danger
11. Living or working in a crowded space
12. Not getting enough exercise
13. Poor nutrition
14. Not getting enough sleep
15. Not enough time to relax
16. Being dissatisfied with your physical appearance
17. Abusing drugs or alcohol, or being close to someone who abuses them

Social and Cultural Causes of Stress

Stress has become a factor in our culture in the last 20 years because of things that were originally designed to make life less stressful. Conveniences such as ATM machines, microwave ovens, and fax machines have made life easier in many ways, but they also have woven an expectation of instant gratification into our culture. And this causes stress.

Here are a few other examples of products and services that were invented to make life more efficient and productive, but which sometimes seem instead to add to stress:

- 24-hour stores and restaurants
- One-hour photo developing
- Drive-thru fast food
- 10-minute oil change
- Web sites, with their instant access to unlimited information
- Catalog and Internet shopping
- Personal computers
- E-mail
- CNN Headline News
- 30-minute pizza delivery

Stress at Work

Almost everyone complains of stress at work these days. It often results from one of the following:

1. Having too much or too little work to do
2. Having to do work that is very complicated and demanding

76

3. Having to do work that is boring and repetitive
4. Having unclear goals and expectations
5. Having to follow changing or confusing procedures
6. Being at a career dead end
7. Working in a company with an impersonal management philosophy

Who Work Stress Affects Most

Stress affects people in every type of work setting.

People at the top of organizations suffer from stress because of excessive workloads, unrealistic expectations, and isolation. The phrase "it's lonely at the top" has some truth to it.

Middle managers often experience stress because they have responsibility for the people who report to them, but lack the control to execute what is expected. With the recent epidemic of corporate downsizing, middle managers have also been given greater and greater workloads. Managers who manage to keep their jobs often feel like they are living in the shadow of termination.

Professionals suffer from their own brand of stress caused by monotony. Doctors, lawyers, and other professionals often perform the same kind of work for many years, resulting in boredom and desperation.

Workers at the lower levels of today's organizations often feel stress caused by boredom and the frustration of dealing with the public. They also may feel less

successful than their coworkers in higher-level jobs and may feel stressed by their lack of status.

Why Workplace Stress Has Increased

1. The nature of work has changed. The fight-or-flight responses to stress are ineffective in response to the stresses of today's life.
2. The workplace has become decentralized. In many places, people no longer work together in one place, but may be scattered around the world or work from home, connected by technology.
3. People change with each generation. Baby Boomers differ from Generation Xers in terms of their values, work ethic, and their definitions of success. These generational differences contribute to stress at work.

How Stress Affects Women

Both genders experience stress. It affects women in some unique ways, however. Here are a few of them:

1. Overall, women are still paid less than men for the same work.
2. Women still face a glass ceiling as they climb the corporate ladder. A recent report stated that only 2% of the members of top management of North American corporations are women.
3. Women who choose to have children are usually responsible for the logistics of child care.
4. Women with children often do more housework when they get home than their husbands do.

5. Compared with men, women with children also tend to experience more guilt feelings about leaving their children to go to work.

In the next newsletter, we will explore ways you can manage stress and keep it from detracting from the quality of your life.

Bob West is a licensed psychologist in Schaumburg. He specializes in working with executives and managers. Call 555-0987 for your free consultation.

Suggested Reading

Jeff Davidson, *The Complete Idiot's Guide to Managing Stress*. New York, NY: Alpha Books, 1997.

J. Barton Cunningham, *The Stress Management Sourcebook*. Los Angeles, CA: Lowell House, 1997.

Peter G. Hanson, *Stress For Success*. New York, NY: Doubleday, 1989.

Peter G. Hanson, *The Joy of Stress*. Kansas City, MO: Andrews & McMeel, 1985.

Psych Update

24. Managing the Stress in Your Life

By Bob West, Ph.D.

In the last newsletter, we discussed what stress is and what causes it. In this issue, you will learn how to manage the stress in your life and protect yourself against it.

Learn to Have Healthy Relationships

This subject could fill an entire book. In the limited space of this newsletter, let's look at the key components of this stress-reducing strategy.

1. **Identify the sources of stress in your relationships.** Write about them in a journal. Make a list of people who cause you stress and explore what the issues are.
2. **Resolve the underlying issues.** For each of the situations identified in step 1, assess what needs to happen to resolve it. Make a list and design a plan to improve the situation.
3. **Learn skills to improve relationships.** Relationship skills are learned. We are not born knowing how to get along well with others, and most of us learned only limited skills from our parents. Identify the skills you need to develop, and make a plan for yourself. You can learn these skills by reading books, taking classes, or working with a therapist.
4. **Avoid toxic people and situations.** Some people have a toxic effect on you. If you can, limit the amount of time you spend with them. Look for opportunities to decline their invitations. When these people are family members, remind yourself that you don't have to feel guilty about avoiding anyone who makes you feel bad about yourself. In work situations, look for ways to rearrange your schedule or your workspace to avoid interacting with such people.
5. **Seek out positive people and situations.** This step is the reverse of the previous step. Look for opportunities to spend more time with people and in situations that make you feel good. Think about people who make you feel good about yourself and look for ways to increase time with them.
6. **Watch what you eat.** Some substances amplify the stress response. These include:

   - **Caffeine** stimulates the release of stress hormones. This increases heart rate, blood pressure, and oxygen to the heart. Ongoing exposure to caffeine can harm the tissue of the heart.

79

- **Refined sugar** and processed flour are depleted of needed vitamins. In times of stress, certain vitamins help the body maintain the nervous and endocrine systems.
- Too much **salt** can lead to excessive fluid retention. This can lead to nervous tension and higher blood pressure. Stress often adds to the problem by causing increased blood pressure.
- **Smoking** not only causes disease and shortens life, it leads to increased heart rate, blood pressure, and respiration.
- **Alcohol** robs the body of nutrition that it might otherwise use for cell growth and repair. It also harms the liver and adds empty calories to the body.

During times of high stress, eat more complex carbohydrates (fruits, vegetables, whole breads, cereals, and beans).

7. **Get moving.** The human body was designed to be physically active. However, in most jobs today, people are sitting down most of the time. They hardly move at all except when it is time for coffee break or lunch. When faced with stressors, we respond with our minds, not our bodies. It is no wonder that many of us have a difficult time responding to stressful events.

Exercise is one of the simplest and most effective ways to respond to stress. Activity provides a natural release for the body during its fight-or-flight state of arousal. After exercising, the body returns to its normal state of equilibrium, and one feels relaxed and refreshed.

8. **Look for ways to let go of tension and anxiety.** Meditation and progressive

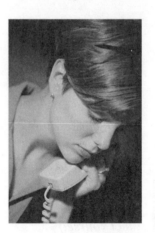

relaxation are two valuable ways to regenerate and refresh yourself. You can purchase meditation and relaxation audio-tapes or record your own. This is especially important because your health and long life depend on minimizing stress and achieving a sense of balance and well-being.

Suggested Reading

Jeff Davidson, *The Complete Idiot's Guide to Managing Stress*. New York, NY: Alpha Books, 1997.

J. Barton Cunningham, *The Stress Management Sourcebook*. Los Angeles, CA: Lowell House, 1997.

Peter G. Hanson, *Stress For Success*. New York, NY: Doubleday, 1989.

Peter G. Hanson, *The Joy of Stress*. Kansas City, MO: Andrews & McMeel, 1985.

Bob West is a licensed psychologist in Schaumburg. He specializes in working with executives and managers. Call 555-0987 for your free consultation.

Today's Counseling

25. What Is Solution-Focused Therapy and How Does It Work?

By Jon Cohen, M.S.

Most types of psychotherapy involve exploring feelings, being validated, finding explanations, exploring wishes and dreams, setting goals, and gaining clarity. Every therapist has unique ways of working with clients, based on his or her personality, training, and views of how people change.

A solution-focused therapist is likely to do the following:

1. Instead of going over past events and focusing on problems, the therapist helps you envision your future *without* today's problems.

2. During the course of therapy (often as few as 3 to 6 sessions), the therapist helps you discover solutions.

3. The therapist encourages you to identify and do *more* of what is already working.

4. The therapist guides you to identify what *doesn't* work and to focus on doing *less* of it.

5. The emphasis is on the future, not the past.

6. SFBT therapists believe that *the client* is the best expert about what it takes to change his or her life.

7. The therapist's role is to help you identify solutions that will remove the barriers to having the life you want.

Solution-Focused Brief Therapy (SFBT) is a process that helps people change by constructing solutions rather than dwelling on problems. This type of therapy tends to be shorter-term than traditional psychotherapy. Steve de Shazer and Insoo Kim Berg of the Brief Family Therapy Center in Milwaukee are the originators of this form of therapy.

The SFBT therapist helps the client identify elements of the desired solution, which are usually already present in the client's life. The client learns to build on these elements, which form the basis for ongoing change. Rather than searching for the causes of the problem, the focus is on defining the changes and making them a reality. The two key therapeutic issues are: (1) how the client wants his or her life to be different, and (2) what it will take to make it happen.

Creating a detailed picture of what it will be like when life is better creates a feeling of hope, and this makes the solution seem possible. The therapist helps the client focus on the future and how it will be better when things change. It is important to develop a set of specific, detailed goals. These goals drive the therapy process and keep it focused and efficient.

Why SFBT Is Usually Short-Term

SFBT therapists don't set out to artificially limit the number of sessions. A good brief therapist will not focus on limiting sessions or time, but rather on helping clients set goals and develop strategies to reach those goals. Focusing on the client's goals and the concrete steps needed to achieve them usually takes less time than traditional therapy, in which the client typically spends many sessions talking about the past and explores reasons and feelings. SFBT therapists aim to provide clients with the most effective treatment in the most efficient way possible so that clients can achieve their goals and get on with their lives. As a result of this focus, the counseling process often requires as few as six sessions.

Types of Problems That SFBT Addresses

Solution-Focused Brief Therapy is an effective way of helping people solve many kinds of problems, including depression, substance abuse, eating disorders, relationship problems, and many other kinds of issues. Since it focuses on the *process* of change rather than on dissecting the problem, more serious issues do not necessarily require different treatment. The SFBT therapist's job is to help

clients transform troubling issues into specific goals and an action plan for achieving them.

In *The Miracle Method,* authors Scott D. Miller and Insoo Kim Berg describe how to create solutions with these steps:

1. State your desire for something in your life to be different.

2. Envision that a miracle happens and your life *is* different.

3. Make sure the miracle is important to you.

4. Keep the miracle small.

5. Define the change with language that is positive, specific, concrete, and behavioral.

6. State how you will start your journey rather than how you will end it.

7. Be clear about who, where, and when, but not why.

Signs That You Should Consider Seeing a Therapist

There are several ways to know when you would be doing yourself a favor by finding a licensed, professional therapist to work with.

1. You've tried several things on your own, but you still have the problem.

2. You want to find a solution sooner rather than later.

3. You have thoughts of harming yourself or others.

4. You have symptoms of depression, anxiety, or another disorder that significantly

interfere with your daily functioning and the quality of your life. For example, you have lost time from work, your relationships have been harmed, or your health is suffering. These are signs that you need the help of a trained, licensed professional.

Suggested Reading

Scott D. Miller and Insoo Kim Berg, *The Miracle Method.* New York, W.W. North & Company, Inc., 1995.

Please pass this newsletter along to a friend. Or call 555-0987 to request additional copies.

Jon Cohen is a licensed counselor and Clinical Director of the Solution-Focused Therapy Center in West Harbor Springs. Call 555-0987 for your free consultation.

Gray's Chronicle

26. Suicide: Warning Signs and Treatment

By Todd Gray, LCSW

It is reported that suicide, the act of deliberately ending one's own life, is a cause of death for about 30,000 people (including 5,000 between the ages of 15 to 24 years old) each year in the United States. Since many suicides are not reported as such, the actual number is most likely much higher. Suicide goes unreported because of its stigma or because family members find it too painful to confront the truth.

The rate of suicide in this country is about 12 per 100,000 people, making it the ninth leading cause of death in the United States during the years from 1993 to 1995. According to the American Association of Suicidology (which studies suicide and its prevention), there are between eight and 20 attempts at suicide for each death from suicide. This means that there are anywhere from 240,000 to 600,000 suicide attempts each year. This rate jumps to 200 attempts for every completed suicide when young people (ages 15 to 24) are involved.

Other Facts about Suicide

- In the U.S., Nevada has the highest rate of suicide.
- More suicides happen in the spring than at other times of the year.
- The most lethal days of the week are Monday and Friday.
- Rich people and poor people alike kill themselves. Suicide is an equal-opportunity killer, and is chosen by people from every group imaginable. The most common victims are white males aged 65 and older.
- More men than women kill themselves, but women are more likely to attempt suicide.
- 60% of people who commit suicide do so with guns.

Why People Commit Suicide

There are many reasons why people kill themselves, and we seldom know why certain individuals choose this route. The following factors seem to play a role in many suicides, but none of them guarantees that a person will end his or her life. Often it is a combination of factors that seem to interact with a person's circumstances; the factors are unique for each person. Some of these factors include:

Clinical depression. This type of depression is much more than just a simple case of the blues; it is severe and debilitating. It may surprise you to know that people who suffer from depression are at the greatest risk for suicide after they have begun treatment and are beginning to feel better. The reason for this is that when a person is severely depressed, they may lack the energy to carry out suicide. When they begin to recover and feel better, their energy begins to return and they may carry it out then.

Alcoholism and drug abuse are associated with a higher suicide rate because these substances impair judgment. Over half of all adolescent suicides and suicide attempts are associated with alcohol. When a person is under the influence of alcohol, he or she has fewer inhibitions and may also think and act in ways that would never happen when sober. Alcoholism and drug abuse also create additional stresses in the lives of users and may result in depression and a tendency toward desperate behavior.

Mental illness. People who have certain disorders, such as schizophrenia, have a higher risk of suicide.

Physical illness, including terminal illness and the illnesses common as people age, is often a factor that contributes to people taking their own lives.

Feeling hopeless is very common among people who commit suicide. Hopelessness may be part of clinical depression, or it may be the result of an illness or other dire circumstance. When a person feels hopeless, he or she feels trapped, and suicide may seem like the only way out.

Anger motivates some people to commit suicide. After a long, unhappy relationship and years of building anger, these people see their suicide as a dramatic way to send a message of retribution.

A **sudden loss** may precipitate suicide in some people. The shock and grief of an enormous loss—of a person or a job— may drive a person to such an extreme.

Experiencing a **scandal** or **extreme embarrassment** leads some people to feel so trapped in their situation that they can think of no other way out.

Suicide Warning Signs

One expert says that eight out of 10 people who kill themselves have given clear warnings that they were considering suicide. While these warning signs can be evident for almost anyone at some point in their life, it is important to be aware of them and take them seriously when you see them.

- Making a threat of suicide, e.g., "I wish I were dead," "I'm going to end it."
- Expressing hopelessness
- Expressing helplessness
- Expressing worthlessness
- Talking about death
- Having previous suicide attempts
- Seeming depressed, moody, or angry
- Having trouble at school or at work
- Abusing alcohol or drugs
- Taking risks
- Withdrawing from other people
- Behaving differently or oddly
- Sleep difficulties
- Loss of appetite
- Giving away prized possessions.
- Suddenly seeming happy after exhibiting several of the behaviors listed above.

Treatment

The treatment for a suicidal person varies, depending on severity and the underlying cause. Treatment can range from immediate hospitalization to weekly psychotherapy with a licensed mental health professional. It may also include antidepressant medication or treatment for drug or alcohol addiction.

What to Do if Someone Is Suicidal

Take action immediately. Depending on the urgency of the situation, call your doctor, hospital, mental health center, suicide hotline, or police emergency number (911).

Suggested Reading

Eric Marcus, *Why Suicide?: Answers to 200 of the Most Frequently Asked Questions About Suicide, Attempted Suicide, and Assisted Suicide.* San Francisco, CA: HarperSanFrancisco, 1996.

Todd Gray is a licensed Clinical Social Worker in Modesto. He specializes in working with people with mood disorders. Call 555-0987 for your free consultation.

Skills for Success

27. Take Charge of Your Life

By Rachel LeMay
Director, Aurora Counseling Associates

It is important to have goals because they are good for your physical and mental health. You can have goals for all areas of your life. Here are a few ideas:

Career	Learning
Clubs	Money
Community	Politics
Contribution	Professional
Emotional	Reading
Family	Relationships
Health	Service
Home	Spiritual
Interests	Travel

What Makes an Effective Goal?

Not all goals are motivating. If a goal is too vague, hard to measure, or impossible to achieve, it will lack effectiveness and ulti-mately be a wasted exercise. Goal statements should be:

- Stated with action verbs
- Specific
- Measurable
- Challenging
- Written down, with completion dates

Effective goals have *all five* ingredients.

The 80/20 Rule

The 80/20 Rule (also known as Pareto's Principle) says that 20% of what we do produces 80% of the results. Here are a few examples:

- 20% of the area in your house requires 80% of the cleaning.
- 20% of the stocks in an investor's portfolio produce 80% of the results.
- 20% of the kids in a class cause 80% of the problems.
- 20% of the books in a bookstore account for 80% of the sales.

You can probably think of a few examples of your own. Note them here:

_____

_____

_____

It's important to remind yourself not to get bogged down on low-value activities, but to stay focused on the high-value 20%.

High-Payoff Planning

High-payoff (HIPO) time is the 20% that produces the desired results. Low-payoff (LOPO) time is the 80% that produces only 20% of the results. The challenge is to *find the HIPO tasks and work on those first.*

The HIPO strategies:
- Setting a deadline increases the chances that you will accomplish a task.
- Setting a specific time to do something increases the chances that you will accomplish it.
- Divide and conquer: Break a task into smaller pieces and it becomes easier to complete.
- Motivate yourself by listing the benefits of completing a task.
- Motivate yourself in another way by rewarding yourself for completing a task.

The LOPO strategies:
- Don't do it at all.
- Do it later.
- Do it with minimum time investment or at a lower standard.

Think of your own life. Can you identify five high-payoff and five low-payoff targets and the activities that contribute directly to each?

_____

_____

_____

_____

_____

Identifying and writing down these items increases the chances that they will be accomplished.

Force Field Analysis

For every goal that you set, there are conditions (forces) that *encourage* its completion. There are also conditions that *discourage* its completion.

The Force Field Analysis process helps you identify two kinds of forces: (1) the forces that are pushing *with* you as you work toward your goal (encouraging forces), and (2) the forces that are pushing *against* you (discouraging forces).

The process of force field analysis (developed by scientist Kurt Lewin) is based on a law of physics that says that when two equal but opposite forces push against one another, there is no movement.

Why is this important to a person working toward a goal? Because a similar dynamic can prevent you from achieving your goal.

The idea here is to *avoid paralysis* and encourage momentum by increasing positive (encouraging) forces and decreasing negative (discouraging) forces. For example:

Goal: Run in a marathon in 2002.
Discouraging forces:
- I haven't exercised regularly for the past five years.
- I tend to start projects and then get bored quickly.
- I live in the Midwest and weather can be a problem.

Encouraging forces:
- I am in good health.
- My neighbor is a runner and has encouraged me to take up the sport.
- My family thinks this is a good idea.

After identifying as many encouraging as discouraging forces, you can map a strategy to build on your strengths—the forces in your favor—and reduce the barriers.

I encourage you to choose a goal of your own and make a list of the encouraging and discouraging forces. This will help you develop an action plan and increase your chances of success.

Your Action Plan

Once you have identified the forces that both favor and discourage the achievement of your goal, it's time to make an action plan. Here is an example:

Force: I haven't exercised regularly for the past five years.

Actions I can take:

1. Start slowly.
2. Map out a plan where I start with a 20-minute walk this Saturday morning.
3. Buy a running magazine.
4. Visit a few running web sites.
5. Straighten up the room where my exercise bike has been serving as a clothes rack. Clear away the junk and move a TV in to encourage me to use the bike every other morning.

Who can help me:

1. My neighbor, the runner.
2. My family members will encourage me. I well tell them that I need this.
3. The woman in the next cubicle started an exercise program last year.

Now it's your turn. Just fill in the blanks.

Force: _____

_____

_____

Actions I can take:

1. _____
2. _____
3. _____
4. _____

Who can help me:

1. _____
2. _____
3. _____
4. _____

Our staff of professional counselors can help you identify goals and a strategy for reaching them. Call 555-8765 today for your free consultation.

News for Daily Life

28. What Is Hypnosis and Can It Help You?

By Megan Salter, M.S.

Hypnosis is a natural, normal, relaxed, and focused state of attention. It is characterized by:

- A feeling of well-being
- Relaxed muscles
- Less sensitivity to pain
- Ability to access memories, both good and bad

Hypnotherapy is the use of hypnosis to enable a person to take control of feelings, behaviors, habits, and self-image. A person who is in a hypnotic state or trance responds to guided imagery and suggestions for new, positive behaviors after the trance is over.

Hypnosis is an entirely natural state of consciousness. It is not the same as one's normal waking state. When people are hypnotized, they are completely awake and alert. They know exactly what is happening during every moment. Their awareness is heightened and focused.

It is not possible to be under someone else's control during hypnosis. People do only what they want to do and are always aware of where they are and what they are doing. They are in control at all times. They become highly receptive to positive suggestions, but only if those suggestions are acceptable. The trance may be stopped at any time, just as we see people sometimes when they are having a daydream.

What Kinds of Issues Is Hypnosis Used For?

A professional therapist with formal training and experience in hypnotherapy can use the experiences from hypnosis to address a wide variety of issues. These are a few examples:

- Eliminating destructive habits
- Building positive habits
- Controlling responses to stress
- Overcoming fear
- Alleviating sexual dysfunction
- Improving performance

Like all psychotherapy, the goal of hypnotherapy is for the client to learn new ways of thinking and behaving in order to take control of his or her life. Hypnosis is not a quick fix or magic cure, but it can be very helpful to a motivated client who is willing to work and take responsibility for change.

What Hypnosis Feels Like

A person may become hypnotized in one of two ways: by listening to another person's voice (either on tape or in person) or by listening to one's own thoughts. The hypnotherapist uses vivid imagery that stimulates the subject's imagination, and makes positive suggestions for new behaviors after the session is over.

Most people find that during a trance, they have more access to their feelings and past memories. The subject's awareness ebbs and flows during this time. Thoughts come and go and there may be parts of the session that he or she won't consciously remember afterward. However, the subconscious mind remembers everything.

People usually awaken from a hypnosis session with very pleasant feelings. There is a sense of well-being and even euphoria.

How Long Does Improvement Take?

Most people say they become aware of the suggestions that were made during hypnosis soon after the first session. The subconscious mind begins to prompt the person for the new thoughts and behaviors immediately. If a hypnosis session is especially intense or if a person has listened repeatedly to a self-hypnosis audiotape, these prompts may be more noticeable and effective. The person's level of motivation also has a major effect on how quickly he or she begins to change for the better.

Does Hypnosis Always Work?

With any goal, people sometimes have a hard time achieving success. There are a few reasons for this. First, the subconscious mind is generally attracted to the behavior that has the strongest emotional charge connected to it. We tend to choose behaviors that make us feel good, even if we know they are bad for

us. This is sometimes why we continue to make the less healthy choice.

A second reason that success seems elusive is because people make the mistake of focusing on negatives rather than positives. If you tell yourself what *not* to do, like trying *not* to smoke or *not* to eat cookies or *not* to be nervous, you will have a hard time succeeding because the mind responds to positives, not negatives. It is more effective to say "I am free of the desire to smoke" or "I enjoy eating watermelon" or "I am calm and confident," and to visualize the details of your goal as if it were happening in the present.

How Hypnosis Works

The *conscious* mind functions mostly like a computer. It is black and white, logical, and reasonable. The conscious mind is where we spend most of our time.

Most people in the American culture learn to disregard their *subconscious* feelings and perceptions because they are viewed as irrational and not based in reality. Still, the subconscious mind is a very powerful force for all of us. It contains the most important elements of our psyches: our dreams, fantasies, and emotions.

These two parts of our minds are quite distinct from one another. The language of the subconscious is imagery and metaphor, which the intellect does not understand. The intellect prefers reason and facts, which the subconscious mind does not comprehend.

There are times in our lives when we are reminded of our powerful subconscious mind. When we face emotional turmoil, loss, or trauma, we may experience the subconscious mind's ability to affect both brain and body. When stress is high, our ability to eat, sleep, talk, and think clearly is often impacted. Even though we thought that we had resolved an important issue, the subconscious creates a symptom or illness as a way of telling us that the feelings have not been resolved.

Healing is a subconscious process, not an intellectual process. You cannot improve your life or heal your pain by telling yourself that you should *get a life* or *move on* or *get it together.* Healing is accelerated when you spend some time in the trance state. In a trance, your sense of self is expanded and your critical, questioning mind is relaxed. This enables you to communicate with your subconscious mind by creating images and symbols and by recreating memories. In the relaxed trance state, you can use your imagination to build a picture of how you want your life to be and describe the steps you will need to take to make it real. When you return to normal waking state, you can continue to focus your mental energy on the images you created when you were in the trance.

_____

Megan Salter is a licensed counselor in Chicago. She specializes in hypnotherapy and family therapy. Call 555-0987 for your free consultation.

Today's Counseling

29. I Have Everything I've Ever Dreamed Of. Why Am I Not Happy?

By Gilda Block, MSW

Signs of Discontent

You don't need a degree in psychology to know when you're off-track, but sometimes it creeps up on you. It can seem like you wake up one day and realize that things are not right. These are a few of the signs:

• You don't want to get out of bed.
• You have a hard time motivating yourself to do routine tasks.
• You have doubts about yourself.
• You feel mildly depressed for days at a time.
• You sometimes overeat and/or use alcohol and drugs to feel better or escape.
• You often feel chronically tired, deenergized, and listless.

• You worry about how you will keep things together.
• You feel bored or restless.
• You wish you were somewhere else.
• You often have headaches, stomach upset, and other body aches and pains.
• You sleep too little or too much.
• You have frequent bad dreams or nightmares.
• You oversleep.
• You complain and nag.

Feeling dissatisfied with your life is not a pleasant experience, but it can lead you in a positive direction. These feelings may be important because they are telling you that your actions are out of synch with your values, goals, or talents.

Rediscover What Is Important to You

Imagine that your life is handed back to you and you are able to do anything you want. What is important to you? What values will direct you? Consider each word on the following list individually. It is not necessary to force-rank them or compare them against each other. Assign a rating to each word:

1 = Critically important to me
2 = Important to me
3 = I can live without it

___ Acceptance by others
___ Accomplishment

I Have Everything I've Ever Dreamed Of. Why Am I Not Happy?

___ Activity

___ Admiration

___ Appreciation

___ Authority

___ Beauty

___ Being liked

___ Being well-paid

___ Calm

___ Casualness

___ Certainty

___ Challenge

___ Choice

___ Comfort

___ Community service

___ Competition

___ Creativity

___ Enjoyment

___ Ethics

___ Excellence

___ Excitement

___ Fame

___ Financial security

___ Fitness

___ Flexibility

___ Fortune

___ Freedom

___ Fulfilling my potential

___ Fun

___ Growth

___ Harmony

___ Health

___ Helping others

___ Honesty

___ Independence

___ Informality

___ Leisure

___ Making a difference

___ Mastery

___ Morality

___ Nature

___ Novelty

___ Originality

___ Peace

___ Personal development

___ Pets

___ Pleasure

___ Popularity

___ Power

___ Prestige

___ Privacy

___ Prosperity

___ Quality

___ Recognition

___ Relaxation

___ Respect

___ Risk

___ Solitude

___ Spirituality

___ Stability

___ Status

___ Stimulation

___ Surprise

___ Time for friends

___ Time for my family

___ Uniqueness

___ Variety

___ Wealth

___ Wisdom

Now make a list that summarizes *your* most important values. If you think of something that isn't listed, feel free to add it.

The final part of this process (and this is a very streamlined version of what is possible) is to compare how you are currently spending your time with your list of most important values. How well do they match each other? What clues can you find that will help you find more satisfaction in your life?

Things that don't match:

_____

_____

_____

_____

_____

What I can do about it:

_____

_____

_____

_____

Suggested Reading

Teri-E Belf and Charlotte Ward, *Simply Live It UP: Brief Solutions.* Bethesda, MD: Purposeful Press, 1995.

Paul and Sarah Edwards, *Finding Your Perfect Work: The New Career Guide to Making A Living, Creating A Life.* New York: Jeremy Tarcher, 1996.

Jennifer Louden, *The Woman's Retreat Book: A Guide to Restoring, Rediscovering, and Reawakening Your True Self.* San Francisco: HarperSanFrancisco, 1997.

Barbara Sher with Barbara Smith, *I Could Do Anything If I Only Knew What It Was.* New York: Delacorte Press, 1994.

Gilda Block is a licensed counselor in Cascade. She specializes in working with older adults and their families. Call 555-0987 for your free consultation.

Monthly Update

30. How to Forgive Another Person for Past Hurts

By Janet Erdman

No one gets through life without being hurt by another person. We all have experienced the pain of a thoughtless remark, gossip, or lie. If you have experienced an unhappy marriage, the devastation of infidelity, or suffered physical or emotional abuse, you know what it feels like to be hurt. It is tempting to hold on to these feelings and build a wall of safety around yourself, but the best way to heal is to forgive the person who hurt you.

What Is Forgiveness?

When you forgive another person, you no longer allow their behavior to cause you anger, pain, bitterness, or resentment. When you choose *not* to forgive, you make the choice to hold on to your feelings of resentment, anger, and pain.

Why Should I Forgive?

Think of forgiveness as a gift that you give to yourself. It is *not* something you do for the person who hurt you. It is a gift to yourself because it enables you to stop feeling painful feelings and pushing others away. Forgiveness frees you from anger and allows you to restore your ability to have close and satisfying relationships with others.

Anger is a poisonous emotion that comes from being hurt. When you are consumed with anger and bitterness, it hurts *you* at least as much as it hurts the person who has harmed you. It is as if you are filled with poison. If these feelings are not resolved, they can begin to eat you up inside. You have two choices: to stay connected to the person who hurt you by keeping these poisonous feelings alive, or to let the feelings go and forgive the person who harmed you. When you withhold forgiveness, think about who is actually being hurt. It is more than likely that the person who is filled with anger and anxiety is you, not the other person.

What Forgiveness Is *Not*

Forgiving another does *not* mean you will never again feel the pain or remember the thing that hurt you. The hurtful experience will be in your memory forever. By forgiving, you are *not* pretending the hurtful behavior never happened. It *did* happen. The important thing is to learn from it while letting go of the painful feelings.

Forgiveness is *not* about right or wrong. It doesn't mean that the person's behavior was okay. You are not excusing their behavior or giving permission for the behavior to be repeated or continued.

When you forgive another, it does *not* mean you wish to continue your relationship with them. This is a separate decision. You can forgive a person and live your life apart from them.

Forgiveness can only take place because we have the ability to make choices. This ability is a gift that we can use it whenever we wish. We have the choice to forgive or not to forgive. No other person can force us to do either.

Steps to Forgiveness

The experience of forgiveness is a process. Since each situation is unique, it is impossible to predict how long it will take or which steps will be the most important to carry out. Here are some ideas for beginning the process:

1. Acknowledge your feelings of anger and hurt. Sometimes it seems like it might be easier to deny the feelings or push them back down, because it hurts to feel them. In the long run, denying these feelings only causes you more pain and actually *prolongs* the hurt.
2. Express your feelings constructively. No matter how badly you were treated or how angry you are, it is never acceptable to harm anyone else. You may need to find a neutral third party to talk to until you feel calmer toward the person who hurt you.
3. Depending on the situation, the person who hurt you may still be a danger to you, physically or emotionally. It is important to protect yourself from being harmed again.
4. At some point, you will see that you are harmed by holding on to feelings of hurt and anger. These feelings can take up space in your psyche and intrude on your sense of well-being. You may feel physically ill. This is when you will be ready to make the decision to stop hurting.
5. Be willing to see the situation from the other person's point of view. This will help you develop compassion, which will eventually replace the feelings of anger. One helpful technique is to write a letter to yourself as if you were the other person. Use his or her words to explain the hurtful things that were done to you. This takes you out of the victim role and helps you restore your power.
6. It is not necessary to know why the hurtful behavior happened. Even if you do learn the reason, you probably won't feel any better. Chances are, the person who harmed you isn't sure why they did it either.
7. Think about the part *you* played in the situation. Don't blame yourself; rather, forgive yourself for the role you played.
8. Recall a time when you caused harm to another person, and that person forgave you. Remember what the guilt felt like. Then, remember what you felt when the other person forgave you. You probably felt grateful and relieved. Remember how this felt and consider giving this same gift to the person who hurt you.

9. Make a list of the actions you need to forgive. Describe the specific actions that caused you harm. State what happened, as objectively as possible.

10. Make a list of the positive aspects of your relationship with the person who hurt you. There must have been something positive, or you wouldn't have participated in it. This helps you regain some perspective and not paint the picture in completely negative terms.

11. Write a letter to the person who harmed you. This letter is for your healing; you do not need to mail it. Describe the positive aspects of the relationship and express your forgiveness for the hurtful behaviors. Express all of your feelings, both positive and negative.

12. If you have decided to end your relationship with the person you have forgiven, have a ceremony to symbolize it. You may wish to burn the letter and the list, or you may visualize some kind of ending.

13. Sometimes the person you need to forgive is *you*. You can begin to forgive yourself by realizing that when you made the mistake, you did not set out deliberately to hurt another person. If you had known how to make better choices, you would have. You did the best you could at the time.

14. Make the forgiveness tangible. You may choose to send the letter to the person you are forgiving or tell a trusted friend what you have done.

Once you have let go of the pain and released yourself form past hurts, you will most likely feel a greater sense of freedom and well-being. Now you are free to move on with your life without bitterness and resentment. You no longer need to look back on your past with anger.

Janet Erdman is the Clinical Manager of Collins Counseling Associates in Algonquin, NY. Call 555-1234 for your free consultation.

Emotional Health Letter

31. Managing Difficult Life Transitions

By Herb Cantor

Life is a process of beginnings and endings. In both life and nature, there are times when things move slowly and don't seem to change very much. Then, suddenly, things change quickly. Moving from August to September, the weather changes gradually at first, and then it seems that suddenly summer is over. It is the same in our lives; transitions are as natural as the changing seasons.

Life transitions are challenging because they force us to let go of the familiar and face the future with a feeling of vulnerability. Most life transitions begin with a string of losses:

- The loss of a role
- The loss of a person
- The loss of a place
- The loss of your sense of where you fit in the world

Any significant loss makes most people feel fearful and anxious. Since your future may now be filled with questions, it is normal to feel afraid. We live in a culture that has taught us to be very uncomfortable with uncertainty, so we are anxious when our lives are disrupted. On the positive side, these transitions give us a chance to learn about our strengths and to explore what we really want out of life. This time of reflection can result in a sense of renewal, stability, and a new equilibrium.

A life transition can be positive or negative, planned or unexpected. Some transitions happen without warning, and they may be quite dramatic, as in cases of accidents, death, divorce, job loss, or serious illness. Other life transitions come from positive experiences such as getting married, going away to college, starting a new job, moving to a new city, or giving birth to a child. Even though events like these are usually planned and anticipated, they can be just as life-altering as the unexpected events. Whether positive or negative, life transitions cause us to leave behind the familiar and force us to adjust to new ways of living, at least temporarily. They can leave us feeling completely unprepared and we may be thrown into a personal crisis, feeling shocked, angry, sad, and withdrawn.

Examples of Life Transitions

Life transitions can include any of the following:

- Accidents
- Buying a house
- Changing jobs
- Divorce

(continued)

- Getting married
- Having a baby
- Leaving for college
- Relocation
- Retirement
- Selling a house
- Serious illness
- Significant loss (of a person, job, pet, or anything important)
- Starting a career

Stages of Life Transitions

Successfully moving through a life transition usually means experiencing the following stages:

1. Experience a range of negative feelings (anger, anxiety, confusion, numbness, self-doubt).
2. Feel a loss of self-esteem.
3. Begin to accept the change.
4. Acknowledge that you need to let go of the past and accept the future.
5. Begin to feel hopeful about the future.
6. Feel increased self-esteem.
7. Develop an optimistic view of the future.

The process of moving through a transition does not always proceed in order, in these nice, predictable stages. People usually move through the process in different ways, often cycling back and forth among the stages.

Coping Skills

Life transitions are often difficult, but they have a positive side, too. They provide us with an opportunity to assess the direction our lives are taking. They are a chance to grow and learn. Here are some ideas that may help make the process rewarding.

Accept that change is a normal part of life. People who have this attitude seem to have the easiest time getting through life transitions. Seeing changes as negative or as experiences that must be avoided makes them more difficult to navigate and less personally productive.

Identify your values and life goals. If a person knows who they are and what they want from life, they may see the change as just another life challenge. These people are willing to take responsibility for their actions and do not blame others for the changes that come along without warning.

Learn to identify and express your feelings. While it's normal to try to push away feelings of fear and anxiety, you will move through them more quickly if you acknowledge them. Make them real by writing them down and talking about them with trusted friends and family members. These feelings will have less power over you if you face them and express them.

Focus on the payoffs. Think about what you have learned from other life transitions. Recall the stages you went through, and identify what you gained and learned from each experience. Such transitions can provide a productive time to do some important self-exploration. They can be a chance to overcome fears and to learn to deal with uncertainty. These can be the gifts of the transition process: to learn more about yourself and what makes you happy and fulfilled.

Don't be in a rush. When your life is disrupted, it takes time to adjust to the new reality. Expect to feel uncomfortable during a transition as you let go of old ways of doing things. Try to avoid starting new activities too soon, before you have had a chance to reflect and think about what is really best for you.

Expect to feel uncomfortable. A time of transition is confusing and disorienting. It is normal to feel insecure and anxious. These feelings are part of the process, and they will pass.

Stay sober. Using alcohol or drugs during this confusing time is not a good idea. It can only make the process more difficult.

Take good care of yourself. Transitions are very stressful, even if they are supposed to be happy times. You may not feel well enough to participate in your normal activities. Find something fun to do for yourself each day. Get plenty of rest, exercise, and eat well.

Build your support system. Seek the support of friends and family members, especially those who accept you without judging you and encourage you to express your true feelings. A time of transition is also an excellent time to seek the support of a mental health professional. He or she can guide you through the transition process in a safe and supportive environment.

Acknowledge what you are leaving behind. This is the first step to accepting the new. Think about how you respond to endings in your life: Do you generally avoid them, like the person who ducks out early on her last day on the job because she can't bear to say good-bye? Or do you drag them out because you have such a hard time letting go? Perhaps you make light of endings, refusing to let yourself feel sad. Before you can welcome the new, you must acknowledge and let go of the old.

Keep some things consistent. When you are experiencing a significant life change, it helps to keep as much of your daily routine consistent as you can.

Accept that you may never completely understand what has happened to you. You are likely to spend a lot of time feeling confused and afraid. This makes most of us very uncomfortable. The discomfort and confusion will pass, and clarity will return.

Take one step at a time. It's understandable to feel like your life has become unmanageable. To regain a sense of power, find one small thing you can control right now. Then break it down into small, specific, concrete steps. Write them down and post them on your computer monitor or mirror. Cross off each step as you accomplish it.

Times of life transitions offer you the chance to explore what your ideal life would look like. When things are in disarray, you can reflect on the hopes and dreams you once had but perhaps forgot about. Take this time to write about them in a journal or talk about them with a trusted friend or therapist. Now is a good time to take advantage of the fork in the road.

> **Please pass this newsletter along to a friend. Or call (your number) to request additional copies.**

Herb Cantor is a licensed psychologist in Northfield, PA. He has been in private practice since 1987 and specializes in helping people through major life changes, including chronic illness. Call 555-1234 for your free, one-hour consultation.

Jeri Schaefer's Update

32. Help! I Need to Make a Decision!

By Jeri Schaefer, M.A.

Many people who come to my office say they have a difficult time making decisions. I have developed a process to help my clients master this skill. I recommend that people follow these four steps:

1. Identify the *real* issue. For example, you are trying to decide which movie to see, but you are having a hard time agreeing. As you talk about it, you realize that the real issue is that you simply want some time to be together in a quiet place where you can talk. Going to a movie does not address this issue.
2. Identify the available options. In the above example, the options might include going to a quiet restaurant, taking a drive, or walking on the beach.
3. Evaluate the available options. Discuss the advantages and disadvantages of each. Evaluate how well each option addresses the real issue.
4. Implement the decision. Make a choice and carry it out.

Even though most people make dozens of important and complex judgments every day, few of us have actually been trained to make good decisions. We started making basic decisions when we were young children, and we continue to follow the same simple process as we get older, even though the issues have become much more complicated.

We learned to make decisions by watching our parents and learning in school. Mostly we learned by trial and error. Our first decisions were pretty simple—to choose pizza or hamburgers, to play softball or soccer, to wear the pink headband or the blue one. These decisions pretty much boiled down to choosing between X and Y.

According to the authors of *Smart Choices: A Practical Guide to Making Better Decisions* (see Reading List), most of us continue to choose between X and Y without making certain that we are addressing the real problem in the first place.

A second common mistake is rushing into a decision, hurrying to get it over with. We rarely step back from the decision and view it in a broader context. While it is more difficult and time-consuming, it is better to take your time and be sure you are seeing the big picture and the key issues.

Strategies for Making Better Decisions

Here are some decision-making tips:

1. Take your time making important decisions. Some situations require a deliberate and careful decision-making process.
2. Once the decision has been made, carry it out without hesitation.

3. If you can, delegate decisions to those who will carry them out. Authors Heller and Hindle (*Essential Manager's Manual*) advise managers always to be on the lookout for ways to push the decision-making process down a level. If you are making decisions for your family, consider how you can involve your kids in the process.
4. Making decisions requires both intuition and logic. It's important to trust your gut, but be sure you are thinking logically.
5. Unless the situation is pretty straightforward, it is a good idea to generate as many ideas as you can. Learn the principles of brainstorming (see box) and throw lots of options into the hopper.
6. Look at the issues from different points of view. How do they look to the different groups they might affect? For example, if a teacher asks his students to wear Native American clothing tomorrow, will the kids' parents have the time to help them prepare on such short notice?
7. Consider the immediate and long-term implications of each solution, including its impact on other people.
8. Consider the worst- and best-case scenarios, as well as the possibilities in between.

Deciding Yourself versus Involving Others

Involving others in your decision-making process helps you avoid the tendency to rush into a decision, hurrying to get it over with. When you take the time to consult others, you force yourself to step back from the situation and see it in a broader context. While it is more difficult and time-consuming, getting the advice and support of others can help you produce better decisions.

Consider these points when seeking *advice:*

1. Determine whom to involve in the process. If it's a simple, low-risk decision, you may not need to involve any one else.
2. If you do ask others for advice and suggestions, be prepared to respond to their input.
3. Determine who will need to approve your decision, and get that approval.

Consider these points when seeking *support:*

1. Think about who might resist your decision, and have a plan to manage that resistance. For example, you want to allow your daughter to have her friends sleep over on a weeknight during the summer, but you expect your husband will object because he has to get up for work the next day and doesn't want his sleep disturbed. Think about how you could plan the evening in a way to avoid disturbing your husband.
2. Identify ways to increase the chances that your decision will be supported. In the sleepover example, you could ask the girls' friends to bring sleeping bags, and set up the basement for them to sleep in.
3. If your decision presents any risks, look for ways to minimize them.

Make This Work for You

Identify a situation in your life right now. Be sure to choose something important and challenging. Apply the steps we have been exploring to this situation.

Rules of Brainstorming

1. Write down the question you are addressing. For example, "Where shall we go on vacation?"
2. Think of as many ideas as you can.
3. Write down every idea, no matter how wild it seems.
4. No one is allowed to judge or evaluate any of the ideas in any way. This includes making faces, rolling eyes, and sighing.
5. The goal is to think of as many ideas as you can. Quantity is more important than quality.
6. After everyone is finished suggesting ideas, take a break.
7. After the break, discuss the ideas and edit the list. A solution will emerge.

Reading List

Hammond, John, Keeney, Ralph, and Raiffa, Howard, *Smart Choices: A Practical Guide to Making Better Decisions.* Harvard Business School Press, 1998.

Heller, Robert and Hindle, Tim, *Essential Manager's Manual.* New York, NY: DK Publishing, 1998.

Jeri Schaefer is a licensed therapist in Tower Lakes. Call 555-1234 for a free telephone consultation.

1. Describe the situation.
2. What is the real issue here?
3. List the pros and cons of each option.
4. What do you need to consider when seeking *advice?*
5. What do you need to consider when seeking *support?*
6. What are the best options?
7. Who needs to be involved?
8. What should be delegated? To whom?
9. What resources would need to be secured?
10. What steps need to be planned, and what is their timing?

The Santangelo Letter

33. You Can Have Excellent Listening Skills

By John Santangelo

Any professional counselor will tell you that one of the biggest problems they see among their clients is poor listening skills. People get into trouble in their relationships because they have not developed their ability to listen and communicate.

Barriers to Effective Communication

There are some good reasons why many people are less-than-effective communicators. These are the most common reasons:

- Lack of skill; not knowing how
- Not taking the time to think through what one wants to say
- Not taking the time to anticipate what another person might be thinking and feeling
- Fear of revealing too much of oneself
- Being afraid of another person's anger
- Not wanting to hurt another person's feelings

Four Key Listening Skills

Listening skills are the building blocks of effective communication. These skills enable you to demonstrate that you are interested in what the other person has to say, as well as hearing and understanding the other person. Four key listening skills are open-ended questions, summary statements, reflective statements, and neutral questions and phrases. They are easy to learn with a little practice.

Open-ended questions begin with *what, why, how do,* or *tell me.*

- These questions get the other person to open up and elaborate on the topic.
- Asking these kinds of questions gets the other person involved by giving him or her a chance to tell what they think or know.
- These questions are designed to encourage the other person to talk.
- They are useful when the other person is silent, or reluctant to elaborate.
- They are also useful in dealing with negative emotions (such as anger or fear), since they help encourage the other person to vent feelings.

Examples of open-ended questions:

"How do you feel about what she said?"
"Tell me all about this new project."
"What do you think about the new offices?"

Summary statements sum up what you hear the other person is saying.

- A summary statement enhances the other person's self-esteem by showing that you were listening carefully.

- It also helps you focus on facts, not emotions.
- It helps the other person clarify his or her own thinking by hearing your summary.
- Summary statements also help you deal with multiple disagreements so you can deal with them one by one.
- They help eliminate confusion by focusing on the relevant facts.
- Summary statements also help you separate the important issues from the trivial.

Examples of summary statements:

"So you're saying you want to go to the library and the bookstore before you decide which books you need. Then you want to go over your choices with me."

"You're saying that you tried your best on this homework assignment, but it was beyond your control."

Reflective statements rephrase what you heard the person say and reflect it back.

- A reflective statement is a way of demonstrating that you were listening carefully.
- It shows the other person that you take them seriously and want to understand what they are feeling.
- It helps you clarify whether you understand what the other person is saying and feeling.

Examples of reflective statements:

"You feel sad because your mother has to leave so soon after such a good visit."

"You're feeling upset because I was late again."

"You sound frustrated that you won't be able to finish the project on time."

Neutral questions and phrases get the other person to open up and elaborate on the topic you are discussing.

- These questions are more focused than open-ended questions.
- They help the other person understand what you are interested in hearing more about.
- They further communication because they help you gain more information.
- When you ask these kinds of questions, you demonstrate to the other person that you are interested and that you are listening.

Examples of neutral questions and phrases:

"Give me some more reasons why we should buy the computer now rather than in January."

"Tell me more about why you want to take this job."

Try Your Hand at Using Listening Skills

Here are some common life situations where good listening skills would come in handy. Read each one and think about which of the four listening skills would help the most. Write an example of what you could say to the other person to validate his or her feelings and encourage further expression of emotion. Check your answers with those on the back page of this newsletter.

1. Your spouse returns from an important business trip. He is very quiet. When you ask him how the trip went, he shrugs his shoulders and says, "Okay."

Which listening skill would be effective in this situation?

What could you say?

2. Your coworker says, "I really wish I didn't have to go to that conference next week. I know I have to, but I wish I could get out of it somehow. I don't like traveling, I hate being away from my family, and I resent having to spend time kissing up to those field people!"

Which listening skill would be effective in this situation?

What could you say?

3. "I wish I could just stay home and garden today," your spouse says.

Which listening skill would be effective in this situation?

What could you say?

4. You are 20 minutes late to pick up your son for a soccer game. There was no way you could let him know you were going to be late. When you arrive, he opens the car door and glares at you. He growls, "I thought you'd be on time for once!"

Which listening skill would be effective in this situation?

What could you say?

5. Your business partner wants to stay in your present office space, which you have outgrown. You want to look for a bigger place. She says, "It makes me so nervous to make such a big commitment! And what if we don't like it in the new place? I think we should just stay where we are."

Which listening skill would be effective in this situation?

What could you say?

Suggested Answers to Listening Skills Exercise

Lots of different listening skills would be effective in each of the five situations. Here are some suggested answers:

1. Open-ended question: "Why don't you tell me about it?"
2. Reflective statement: "You sound frustrated and upset about having to go to the conference."
3. Reflective statement: "You really love gardening because it's so relaxing."
4. Reflective statement: "You are really upset with me for being late, aren't you?"
5. Summary statement: "You're afraid that we'll be in over our heads and will think it's a mistake."

Suggested Reading

Burley-Allen, Madelyn, *Listening: The Forgotten Skill* (2nd edition). New York, NY: John Wiley & Sons, 1995.

Santangelo Associates is a nonprofit counseling center in Wauconda, GA. Call 555-1234 for information.

You Can Do It

34. 12 Rules for Constructive Communication

By Melody Sanchez

Destructive communication erodes self-esteem and harms relationships. Such communication patterns may be destructive, but, sadly, plenty of people fall into the trap of indulging in them. If you and your relationship partners follow these rules and steer clear of the traps of destructive communication, you will almost certainly feel better about each other and your relationship.

1. *Use I-messages instead of You-messages.* You-messages sound blaming and accusing. With an I-message, you can convey the same message without sounding blaming. For example:

You-message: "You left the dishes in the sink again."

I-message: "When you don't clean up after yourself, I feel taken advantage of."

2. *Communicate the entire message.* According to McKay et al. in their excellent book *Couple Skills* (see Suggested Reading), complete messages include four components:

Observations: neutral statements of fact

Thoughts: your own opinions and beliefs

Feelings: descriptions of your emotions

Needs: a statement of what you need or want from the other person

Here is an example of a complete message: "The weekend is coming up. I hope we can go to the movies together. I would like to spend some time with you."

An incomplete message leaves out one or more of these components. It might sound like this: "I hope we can go to the movies this weekend." There isn't really anything wrong with this statement, but the first one is more complete and will more likely result in the speaker getting what he or she wants.

3. *Don't use your feelings as weapons.* Just describe what you are feeling as objectively as possible, not aggressively. Be as specific as possible and keep your voice under control. For example:

Objective: "I felt really hurt when you said that I probably wouldn't pass the bar the first time."

Aggressive: (*yelling*) "You are such an idiot! How dare you insult me like that!"

4. *Use specific language.* When you have a complaint, be specific. For example, "I'm upset that you left the food out on the table" is clearer than saying, "Thanks for the mess you left me." The first statement is less likely to produce defensiveness and leaves little room for misunderstanding.

5. *Focus on the problem, not the person.* Consider how different these two statements sound:

"You are such a complete slob."

"I wish you would take your stuff upstairs."

Attacking someone's personality or character—rather than a specific behavior—is different from simply expressing a complaint. A complaint focuses on a specific action. Criticism is more blaming and more global. It sounds like this: "You always screw the budget up. Can't you do anything right?"

Behavior like this is damaging to a relationship because:

- Criticism is *destructive* rather than *constructive.*
- It involves blame.
- Criticisms are global and tend to be generalizations (*you always, you never,* etc.).
- Criticisms attack the other person personally.
- It feels overwhelming to be on the receiving end.

6. *Stop bringing up ancient history.* It's more constructive to focus on the issue at hand, not bring up past hurts. When you are upset with your partner and add past issues to

the discussion, it can only escalate the conflict. It feels unfair and can never be productive. If you still have feelings about past issues, it is important to resolve them and move on, not use them as weapons every time you have a disagreement with your partner.

7. *Watch out for mixed messages.* Keep your statements clean, avoiding the temptation to mix compliments and complaints. For example, let's say that you meet your friend at a cocktail party. You think she looks nice, but her dress seems a little too provocative.

Straight message: "You look very nice tonight."

Mixed message: "You look so pretty. I would never have the nerve to wear that."

8. *Pay attention to your body language.* Your words are only part of the message you communicate. If you say "How nice to see you" while frowning, your message becomes unclear. Think about what message you want to convey and be sure that your body is in harmony with it. Watch out for things like these:

- Rolling your eyes
- Crossing your legs and arms
- Tapping your foot
- Clenching your teeth

9. *Pay attention to your emotions and keep from becoming overwhelmed.* If you are calm, you are less likely to say things you'll later regret, things that could be destructive to your relationship. You will be less likely to become defensive and shut your partner out. Examples of ways to calm yourself and keep from getting carried away with emotion include the following:

- Pay attention to your physical responses. Is your heart racing? Are you breathing faster? If you are, take a time-out.
- Leave the room. Go for a drive. Do something relaxing. Listen to music or do relaxation exercises.
- Make a conscious effort to calm yourself down. Say things to yourself like:

  "I'm very upset right now, but it'll be okay. I still love her."

  "Even though we disagree, we still have a good relationship."

  "We can work this out. We're partners."

10. *Resolve negative feelings.* If you have bad feelings about your partner, take steps to resolve them. Don't let them grow into feelings of contempt. When you engage in behavior (verbal or nonverbal) that conveys a lack of respect, you are placing your relationship in serious danger. This includes obvious abuse, and also insults, making faces, and name-calling. Any relationship that is plagued by abusiveness and negativity will have a very difficult time surviving.

11. *Don't be defensive.* It is understandable to react defensively when you are in a conflict situation, but it can be dangerous to a relationship. Defensiveness tends to escalate the conflict and does nothing to resolve it. Some examples of defensive behavior include:

- Denying responsibility (*I did not!*)
- Making excuses (*I couldn't help it; traffic was awful*)
- Ignoring what your partner says and throwing a complaint back (*Yeah, well, what about the mess you left yesterday?*)

- Saying *Yes, but . . .*
- Whining
- Rolling your eyes or making a face

12. *Don't shut down.* In *Why Marriages Succeed or Fail and How You Can Make Yours Last* (see Suggested Reading), author John Gottman describes the dangers of shutting out the other person. He calls this behavior *stonewalling* and says that it means refusing to communicate, storming out of the room, or any kind of withdrawing. When a person is stonewalling, communication is impossible because he or she is refusing to participate. When it becomes a regular pattern of communication, stonewalling is very damaging to a relationship.

Please pass this newsletter along to a friend. Or call (your number) to request additional copies.

Suggested Reading

Gottman, John, *Why Marriages Succeed or Fail and How You Can Make Yours Last.* New York, NY: Fireside Books, 1994.

McKay, Matthew, Fanning, Patrick, and Paleg, Kim, *Couple Skills: Making Your Relationship Work.* Oakland, CA: New Harbinger Publications, 1994.

Melody Sanchez is a licensed social worker in private practice in Big Bear, Michigan. She specializes in coaching people to become better communicators. Call 555-1234 for your free initial consultation.

Client Outreach News

35. You Can Build Your *People Skills*

By Sarah Wadhwa

How would you like to get along even better with others in your personal relationships and in the workplace? Getting along well with people sounds kind of general and is difficult to do much about, so let's break it down into some manageable and specific skills. By building the following skills, you will get along well with others:

1. **Build others' self-esteem.**
2. **Show empathy for others.**
3. **Encourage people to cooperate with each other.**
4. **Communicate assertively.**

(*continued*)

5. **Ask productive questions and demonstrate listening skills.**
6. **Respond productively to emotional statements.**

People skills (which are also known as *emotional intelligence*) can be thought of as six specific skills. Let's take a brief look at each one.

1. *Build others' self-esteem.* When you are in a situation where you are made to feel good about yourself, you feel good. You can do the same with others by doing the following kinds of things:

    a. Make eye contact with others.
    b. Call others by their names.
    c. Ask others their opinions.
    d. Compliment others' work.
    e. Tell people how much you appreciate them.
    f. Write notes of thanks when someone does something worthwhile.
    g. Make people feel welcome when they come to your home or workplace.
    h. Pay attention to what is going on in people's lives. Acknowledge milestones and express concern about difficult life situations such as illness, deaths, and accidents.
    i. Introduce your family members to acquaintances when you meet them in public.

j. Encourage your loved ones to explore their talents and interests.

k. Share people's excitement when they accomplish something.

l. Honor people's needs and wants.

m. Take responsibility for your choices and actions, and expect others to do the same.

n. Take responsibility for the quality of your communications.

2. *Show empathy for others.* Empathy means recognizing emotions in others. It is the capacity to put yourself in another person's shoes and understand how they view their reality and how they feel about things.

   Being aware of our emotions and how they affect our actions is a fundamental ability in today's people-intense workplaces. People who are cut off from their emotions are unable to connect with people. It's like they are emotionally tone-deaf.

   No one wants to work with such people because they have no idea how they affect others. You have probably met a few people who fit this description.

3. *Encourage people to cooperate with each other.* Whether you are managing a family or a work group, there are some specific things you can do to create an environment where others work together well:

   a. Don't play favorites. Treat everyone the same. Otherwise, some people will not trust you.

   b. Don't talk about people behind their backs.

   c. Ask for others' ideas. Participation increases commitment.

d. Follow up on suggestions, requests, and comments, even if you are unable to carry out a request.

e. Check for understanding when you make a statement or announcement. Don't assume everyone is with you.

f. Make sure people have clear instructions for tasks to be completed. Ask people to describe what they plan to do.

g. Reinforce cooperative behavior. Don't take it for granted.

4. *Communicate assertively.* Assertive communication is a constructive way of expressing feelings and opinions. People are not born assertive; their behavior is a combination of learned skills. Assertive behavior enables you to:

   a. Act in your own best interests.

   b. Stand up for yourself without becoming anxious.

   c. Express your honest feelings.

   d. Assert your personal rights without denying the rights of others.

   Assertive behavior is different from passive or aggressive behavior in that it is:

   a. Self-expressive

   b. Honest

   c. Direct

   d. Self-enhancing

   e. Constructive, not destructive

   Assertive behavior includes both *what* you say and *how* you say it.

5. *Ask productive questions and demonstrate listening skills.* Listening skills help you show that you are hearing and understanding another person and are interested in what he or she has to say.

6. *Respond productively to emotional statements.* A communication skill called *active listening* is especially useful in emotional situations because it enables you to demonstrate that you understand what the other person is saying and how he or she is feeling about it. Active listening means restating, in your own words, what the other person has said. It's a check of whether your understanding is correct. This demonstrates that you are listening and that you are interested and concerned.

Active listening responses have two components:

a. Naming the feeling that the other person is conveying

b. Stating the reason for the feeling

Here are some examples of active listening statements:

"Sounds like you're upset about what happened at work."

"You're annoyed by my lateness, aren't you?"

"You sound really stumped about how to solve this problem."

"It makes you angry when you find errors on Joe's paperwork."

"Sounds like you're really worried about Wendy."

"I get the feeling you're awfully busy right now."

Actively listening is *not* the same as agreement. It is a way of demonstrating that you intend to hear and understand another's point of view.

The ability to get along well with people in your personal relationships and in the workplace is a set of learned skills. No one is born knowing how to build others' self-esteem, show empathy, encourage cooperation, communicate assertively, ask productive questions, or respond productively to emotional statements. These skills can be learned and developed with some practice. By taking the time to develop these skills, you will be able to build better relationships at home and at work.

Sarah Wadhwa is the Manager of Client Services at the Family Counseling Center in Deer Park, WI. Visit www.ABCD.com to learn about the Center's services, or call 555-1234 for a free introductory session.

NEWS FOR FAMILIES

36. 29 Ways to Keep Your Relationship Tuned Up

By Mark Chan, Ph.D.

Why do some relationships last forever and others fall apart? Here are some ways you can make your partner feel appreciated again and prevent your relationship from becoming a casualty.

1. Treat your partner as you would your boss, best friend, or best customer.

2. Think about what your partner wants and give it to him or her.

3. Think of ways you can do the unexpected and be thoughtful. Remember how you acted when you wanted to win your partner over.

4. Pay attention to your appearance. Dress nicely; get into shape.

5. Express your thoughts carefully. Being married doesn't give anyone permission to let it all hang out.

6. Spend regular time together alone.

7. Look for ways to compliment your partner.

8. Hug when you say hello and goodbye. It feels good and it makes people feel loved.

9. Learn and practice communication skills. Relating successfully to another person requires a set of skills that can be learned.

10. Be polite. Just because you are married doesn't mean you can forget your manners.

11. When you want something, say please.

12. When your partner does something for you, say thank you.

13. When your partner comes home after a day at work, greet her at the door and say hello. Ask how her day went.

14. When your partner leaves for work in the morning, say goodbye and "I love you" or "Have a good day."

15. When your partner faces a challenge at work during the day, ask how it went when you get home.

16. During your evening meal together, avoid the temptation to watch television

114

or read the paper or mail. Look at your partner and have a conversation.

17. If you want to make plans that affect how your partner will be spending time, check with him first and make sure it's convenient.

18. When you ask your partner a question, make eye contact and listen to the answer.

19. When you disagree with something your partner says, pay attention to your response. Do you express your opinion without putting her down? You can express your opinion assertively rather than aggressively. For example, you can say, "I have another opinion. I think we should wait until spring to have the walls painted," rather than, "That's silly! We should wait until spring."

20. Pay attention to how much of your side of the conversation is asking questions versus making statements. If you tend to be the dominant one, ask more questions.

21. Ask open-ended questions to encourage your partner to open up and talk. Open-ended questions begin like this:

    a. Tell me about . . .
    b. What do you think of . . .
    c. What was it like when . . .

22. Have you become passive with your partner because that's the easiest way to avoid conflict? Over time, this is not a good idea. You will inevitably begin to build up feelings of resentment because you are stifling your feelings, thoughts, and opinions. If you think you are choosing passive behavior too often, think

about discussing it with your partner and asking him to help you be more assertive.

23. Researchers have found that people whose marriages last the longest have learned to separate from their families of origin (their own parents and siblings) and have appropriate, healthy boundaries. They value and honor their own privacy and separateness as a couple. This means they have regular, appropriate contact with their extended family, but that it is not excessive or stifling. How do you compare?

24. Check your communication with your partner and beware of using "You" messages. These are statements that begin with *you*. For example:

    You need to come home by 6:00 tonight.
    You shouldn't do that.
    You should call me from the office and
    tell me when you'll be home.
    Here is what you ought to do.

    "You" messages are damaging because they make the other person feel bad or disrespected. It feels like you are talking down to him or her.

25. If you want to demonstrate to your partner that you respect and esteem him or her, try speaking with "I" messages instead. When you start your statement with "I," you are taking responsibility for the statement. It is less blameful and less negative than the "you" message.

    You can use this formula: Your feelings + Describe the behavior + Effect on you. This is how an "I" message sounds: *When I heard that you'd planned a weekend up north, I was confused about why you hadn't asked me first, so I could be sure to get the time off.* It takes some practice and you have to stop and think about what you are going to say, but your marriage deserves to be handled with care.

26. Make a list of your partner's positive qualities. Share them with him and tell her why you think each is true.

27. Ask your partner to do the same for you.

28. Respect each other's private space. Over time, many couples let this slide.

29. As the years pass, many couples begin to feel like they are living in the same house, but have parallel lives. Their paths cross in fewer places. What is the trend in your relationship and what do you want to do about it?

_____

Mark Chan is a licensed psychologist in Escondido. He specializes in working with couples and families. Call 555-0987 for your free consultation.

Food for Thought

37. Dealing with the Emotional Impact of Infertility

By Paula Alexander, LCSW

Infertility is a medical problem that results in the inability to conceive a child or carry a pregnancy to full term. A couple is usually diagnosed as infertile after one year of frequent, unprotected, sexual intercourse.

It is estimated that 10 to 15% of couples are infertile. About 35% of infertility cases can be traced to physical problems of the woman and 35% have causes in the man. In the remaining 30% of cases, infertility is either unexplained or is caused by problems in both partners.

Why Infertility Can Be Devastating

The inability to have children can be one of the greatest challenges that a person or couple will ever face. It affects people emotion-ally, physically, and financially. It can place tremendous stress on a couple's relationship and on their relationships with family and friends.

On a physical level, the experience of being examined and tested monthly, weekly, or even daily is embarrassing, exhausting, and very expensive. Medications often have side effects, and daily injections may be required. Surgery is often necessary, and sometimes several procedures are needed.

As the process continues over months and years, the couple's privacy is invaded time and again, physically and emotionally. One or both of the partners learn to put aside their feelings as they lie on the examining table, have fluids taken, or give sperm for the tenth, twentieth, or fiftieth time.

At the same time, family, friends and coworkers are waiting to see if this month will bring good news. The couple becomes used to hearing, "Anything new?" with an expectant smile. They also hear comments like, "Maybe you should take a month off and just relax," or "A vacation would do you good" or "This sounds like a good problem. At least you can have fun trying." To make it even worse, throughout this experience, the couple regularly hears of others who have become pregnant. In fact, it sometimes seems as if the whole world is pregnant.

These experiences often make the infertile person feel like a failure. The feelings come up each time there is a treatment failure or when yet another friend or acquaintance announces a pregnancy.

After each expensive procedure or round of treatment, when no pregnancy results, the disappointment turns to devastation. Many infertile people become depressed and anxious. The strain in the marriage and among family members sometimes becomes unbearable. The self-esteem of one or both partners plummets. They often feel lonely, sad, and angry. The long series of disappointments that many experience can cause a numbing effect, and depression can result. If one partner has the medical problem that is causing the infertility, he or she often feels guilty and may even offer the other a divorce. At the same time, the infertile person may fear that the other partner will leave the relationship. All of these changes can make people feel emotionally distant and needing to avoid intimacy.

Some people cut themselves off from friends and family. They look for ways to avoid attending social gatherings and family events, fearing that they will be subjected to discussions about pregnancy, children, or infertility. Socializing with friends and family who have children or who are pregnant is a special challenge. Sometimes these feelings are intensified, especially for women, when they are taking large doses of drugs that can affect their emotions.

Emotional Self-Care during Infertility

Almost no one expects to be infertile. Most people think they will grow up, get married, and have children, just like everyone else around them. So when a couple learns that they are infertile, they are often surprised at how devastated they feel. After all, they rea-son, they don't have cancer or a deadly disease (in most cases); it's *just* infertility. So why do they feel so badly? Most couples gradually come to realize that it *is* a distressing experience. Many eventually seek the help of a team of professionals, realizing that it is a good idea to create a support network and take advantage of the help that is available.

When one or both partners start to feel the impact of infertility, it can be a good idea to seek the services of a mental health professional, especially one who has experience working with the issues of infertility. Since these issues are so complex, it is important to find a counselor who has experience and training in dealing with the impact on individuals, couples, and families. Many couples also find relief in support groups where they can meet regularly with other infertile couples, share experiences, and support each other. Such groups are offered through organizations like RESOLVE, a national infertility support organization. RESOLVE also provides referrals to medical practitioners who specialize in infertility. Visit www.resolve.org for information.

Infertility is primarily a medical problem, but during treatment it is important to address the emotional implications of infertility. Joining a support group or seeing a qualified counselor is especially important at any of the following points:

- When you begin a new phase of your treatment

- After a course of treatment has failed

- When you are faced with difficult decisions about treatment

- When you are thinking about options such as surrogacy, egg or sperm donation

- When you are considering stopping medical treatment

- When you are thinking about adopting

- When one or both of you have troubling feelings that won't go away

- When you experience strained relationships with your partner, friends, or family

- When you avoid being with others because of the infertility

Although a mental health professional cannot influence the outcome of the medical treatment, he or she can help the couple get through the process by helping them communicate better with each other and gain support from family and friends.

Paula Alexander is a Licensed Clinical Social Worker in Belmont Shores. She specializes in working with people who have infertility and adoption issues. Call 555-0987 for your free consultation.

A Better Life

38. How Divorce Impacts Families

By Tanya Brown, M.A.

As a licensed mental health professional, I work with many individuals, couples, and families who are affected by divorce. I see the devastating effects that breakups can have and am dedicated to helping people develop the skills to cope with experiences like divorce.

Major Disruptions

The decision to divorce causes major changes in the lives of all family members. Some upheaval is inevitable. The main trouble areas are:

1. **Financial:** Money becomes a huge problem for most people. The cost of a divorce is extremely high, and two households cost more than one.
2. **Career:** Being less focused at work and spending time away from the job for divorce-related appointments takes its toll.
3. **Logistics:** Running your home is more difficult because you no longer have a partner to help with daily chores.
4. **Emotional:** Most people have periods of depression, sadness, anger, and fatigue.

Lots of Feelings

People who are experiencing the breakup of their marriage can expect to have a wide variety of feelings. Some call it "the crazy time" and there is even a book about divorce with this title. The following complaints are common:

- Poor concentration
- Nightmares
- Sleep problems
- Fatigue
- Mood swings
- Feeling tense
- Nausea
- Gaining/losing weight
- Feeling nervous
- Somatic complaints

Divorce profoundly affects children. In *Surviving the Breakup,* author Judith Wallerstein describes the experience of 60 divorcing families. She outlines the following key issues for children of divorcing families:

Fear: Divorce is frightening to children, and they often respond with feelings of anxi-

120

ety. Children feel more vulnerable after a divorce because their world has become less reliable.

Fear of abandonment: One-third of the children in Wallerstein's study feared that their mother would abandon them.

Confusion: The children in divorcing families become confused about their relationships with their parents. They see their parents' relationship fall apart and sometimes conclude that their own relationship with one or both parents could dissolve, as well.

Sadness and yearning: More than half of the children in the Wallerstein study were openly tearful and sad in response to the losses they experienced. Two-thirds expressed yearning, for example: "We need a daddy. We don't have a daddy."

Worry: In Wallerstein's study, many children expressed concern about one or both of their parents' ability to cope with their lives. They wondered if their parents were emotionally stable and able to make it on their own.

Over half of the children expressed deep worries about their mothers. They witnessed their mothers' mood swings and emotional reactions to the events in the family. Some children worried about suicide and accidents.

Feeling rejected: Many children who experience a parent moving out of the home feel rejected by the parent. The parent is usually preoccupied with problems and pays less attention to the child than in the past. Many children take this personally and feel rejected and unlovable.

Loneliness: Since both parents are preoccupied with their problems during the divorce process, they are less able to fulfill their parenting roles with their chil-

dren. The children may feel like their parents are slipping away from them. If the father has moved away and the mother has gone off to work, the children often feel profound loneliness.

Divided loyalties: The children may (accurately) perceive that the parents are in a battle with each other. The children feel pulled in both directions and may resolve the dilemma by siding with one parent against another.

Anger: Children in divorcing families experience more aggression and anger. It is often directed toward the parents, expressed in tantrums, irritability, resentment, and verbal attacks. Many children see the divorce as a selfish act and feel very resentful about the resulting destruction of their lives.

More than one-third of the children in Judith Wallerstein's study showed acute depressive symptoms such as sleeplessness, restlessness, difficulty in concentrating, deep sighing, feelings of emptiness, compulsive overeating, and various somatic complaints.

The symptoms that many children may have during the divorce process either moderate or disappear within 18 months after the breakup. Of the symptoms that remain, the most common are:

1. **Manipulative behavior** was reported by about 20% of the teachers of the children in Wallerstein's study.

2. **Depression** was diagnosed in 25% of the children and adolescents. The symptoms of depression in children include:

   • Low self-esteem
   • Inability to concentrate
   • Sadness
   • Mood swings

- Irritability
- Secretiveness
- Isolation
- Self-blame
- Eating disorders
- Behaving perfectly
- Being accident-prone
- Stealing
- Skipping school
- Underachieving at school
- Sexual acting out

You should consider finding a therapist to work with if most of the time you feel:

- Alone
- Depressed
- Numb
- Exhausted
- Isolated
- Hopeless
- Overwhelmed by your children
- Overwhelmed by your feelings
- You are sleeping too much or too little
- Worried
- Anxious
- Afraid

My next newsletter will include a list of 36 survival strategies for people who are experiencing divorce.

Please pass this newsletter along to a friend. Or call 555-0987 to request additional copies.

Suggested Reading

William Bridges, *Transitions: Making Sense of Life's Changes*. New York, Addison-Wesley, 1980.

Marjorie Engel and Diana Gould, *The Divorce Decisions Workbook*. New York, McGraw Hill, 1992, page 109.

Abigail Trafford, *Crazy Time: Surviving Divorce and Building A New Life*. New York, HarperCollins, 1992.

Judith Wallerstein and Joan Berlin Kelly, *Surviving The Breakup: How Children and Parents Cope With Divorce*. New York, Basic Books, 1980.

Tanya Brown is a licensed Marriage and Family Therapist in Chicago. She specializes in working with people who have eating disorders, addictions and PTSD. Call 555-0987 for your free consultation.

A Better Life

39. Divorce Recovery Strategies

By Tanya Brown, M.A.

As a licensed mental health professional, I work with many individuals, couples, and families who are affected by divorce. I have developed this list of survival strategies for people who are experiencing divorce. If you or someone you love is in this situation, I hope these ideas will help you.

1. Take your time as you adjust to your changed life circumstances. Recognize that you are going through a major life transition that cannot be rushed.

2. Set up temporary arrangements to help you get through the changes involved in your divorce process.

3. You will often feel frustrated. Avoid the temptation of acting for the sake of acting just because it gives you a temporary feeling of being in control.

4. When you feel uncomfortable, slow down and identify what you are feeling and why.

5. Don't force any more changes on yourself than are necessary.

6. Explore both the benefits and costs of your new life.

7. Think about the future. In your journal, explore the question, "What is waiting to happen in my life now?"

8. Remember to ask yourself, "What am I supposed to learn from this?"

9. Protect yourself against the inevitable forgetfulness and absent-mindedness which many divorcing people report. Make a list of important account numbers, telephone numbers, and the like, and keep them in a safe place.

10. Watch out for too many changes in your life as you recover from the divorce and the changes in your life circumstances. Change causes stress, and you have enough right now.

11. Let people help you.
    - If it's impossible to reciprocate, say so.
    - People know that your life isn't like it used to be.
    - Don't let your inability to reciprocate prevent you from accepting what people willingly offer.

12. Let go of your need for perfection. You will not survive emotionally unless you lower your expectations.

13. Develop your ability to be flexible and find creative ways to solve problems.

14. Learn to set priorities. Do the most important things first.

15. Trust your gut feelings. Pay attention to your instincts and act on them.

16. Simplify everything in your life. You cannot afford to keep it complicated.

17. Find an outlet for your anger. If a friend is not available, look for a minister, rabbi, or professional counselor. If money is an issue, look for a therapist who will see you for a low fee.

18. Teach yourself to let go of guilt. You don't have time for it and it's not necessary.

19. Focus on issues you have control over. If something is beyond your control, don't waste your emotions on it.

20. Create a ceremony to acknowledge your divorce.

21. Learn to be assertive. You can't say yes to every request, whether it is from your family members or people in the community who want your time and resources. If you give it all away, you will have nothing left for yourself.

22. Find ways to take care of your body. Get regular checkups and make time to exercise. You need rest now more than ever. Watch your alcohol intake.

23. Find someone who will listen to you. Sometimes you have to ask, for example, "I need a sounding board right now. Can I have 15 minutes of your time?"

24. Rent a sad movie and let yourself cry (when the kids aren't around). Crying allows you to release the sadness that you are sure to feel.

25. Do at least one fun thing for yourself every week.

26. In your private journal, make a list of all the things you're afraid of.

27. In your private journal, make a list of all the things you worry about.

If you have children:

28. Manage your own emotions so you will be able to help your child manage his or her struggle.
    - Learn as much as you can about how children respond to divorce and life in a single-parent home.
    - Do not expect your child to respond the same way you do.
    - Take your child's developmental stage into consideration when responding to his or her behavior.

29. Make it okay for your children to talk to you about their feelings.

30. Keep appropriate boundaries.
    - Don't give in to the temptation to let your child take care of you.
    - Let your children be children.
    - Avoid burdening them with your feelings and the facts of the divorce.
    - Find another adult to be your sounding board.

31. Even though you may be unable to be present as much as in the past, your children still need adult supervision. Look for ways for other adults to look in on your kids when they are home alone, even when they are teenagers.

32. Just because your child appears to be handling his or her emotions well, don't assume that he or she is okay. Some kids respond to divorce by becoming overly responsible or by closing down their emotions. They may need to hear, "Tell me how you're feeling."

33. While it is important to listen and accept your children's feelings, it is equally important to set limits on behavior.

34. Keep a private journal where you express your feelings. Be sure to keep it in a private place where your children won't find it. A journal provides a place to express anger, sadness, loneliness, and fear—all of those feelings you feel every day as a single parent.

35. Remind yourself that recovering from divorce will take time. Your recovery will happen on its own schedule, and it will happen. You will get through this intact.

36. Get together with other single-parent families. Sharing times with people facing similar issues can make you feel normal.

Please pass this newsletter along to a friend. Or call 555-0987 to request additional copies.

Suggested Reading

William Bridges, *Transitions: Making Sense of Life's Changes*. New York, Addison-Wesley, 1980.

Marjorie Engel and Diana Gould, *The Divorce Decisions Workbook*. New York, McGraw Hill, 1992, page 109.

Abigail Trafford, *Crazy Time: Surviving Divorce and Building A New Life*. New York, HarperCollins, 1992.

Judith Wallerstein and Joan Berlin Kelly, *Surviving The Breakup: How Children and Parents Cope With Divorce*. New York, Basic Books, 1980.

Tanya Brown is a licensed Marriage and Family Therapist in Chicago. She specializes in working with people who have eating disorders, addictions and PTSD. Call 555-0987 for your free consultation.

Today's Counseling

40. Managing Today's Stepfamily

By Janet Asher, M.S.

If you are a member of a stepfamily, you know how difficult it can be to integrate all of the new members and adjust to the new boundaries and rules. The following ideas may help you make a successful transition during this challenging process.

Have patience. Establishing new families takes time. Just because you love your new partner, it is unrealistic to think that you will automatically love his or her children. It is equally unrealistic to expect that your new partner's children will instantly love you. It can be difficult to accept that even though you wish to have a relationship with your stepchildren, they may not be ready for a relationship with you.

Expect to adjust. With proper help and guidance, children can recover from family disruption. All children experience a difficult adjustment period following a divorce or remarriage. It takes time, patience, and perhaps some professional assistance, but most children are able to regain their emotional bearings. It is critical that the adults manage their own emotional recovery in order to help the children adjust without trauma.

If you are part of a part-time stepfamily, you may need a longer adjustment period. All relationships take time to grow and develop. When stepchildren see you less often, you have less time to get to know each other. This is why it may take a part-time stepfamily longer to move through the adjustment process.

Don't expect your new family to be like your first family. If you expect that your stepfamily will be just like the family of your first marriage, you are setting yourself up for frustration. Your new family will have its own unique identity and will evolve in its own special way.

Expect confusion. Forming a stepfamily is a confusing time for everyone. Think about how confusing it is for a child to become part of two new families. All of the family members—parents and children—must learn to understand the new structure and learn to navigate the boundaries.

Allow time for grieving. Stepfamilies begin with an experience of loss, and everyone needs to grieve. The adults' losses are not the same as those of the children, and both must be respected. Adults grieve the following losses:

- The loss of a partner
- The loss of a marriage relationship
- Lost dreams of the way they thought it would be

- They must adjust to changes that result from the divorce or death (moving to a new house, starting a new job, adjusting to changes in lifestyle, etc.)

Children grieve, too. Their losses are usually different from those of their parents:

- They may now be living with one parent instead of two.
- They may have less time with one or both parents during times of dating and remarriage.
- There may be less stability in their homes.
- They must adjust to changes that result from the divorce or death. (They may have a new place to live and go to a new school; they may have lost friends in this process.)
- They have lost the fantasy of how they wanted their family to be.

Children have an especially difficult time resolving their grief when their parents are hostile with one another, when one or both of their parents remarry, and if they have trouble accepting their new stepparents.

Acknowledge the absent parent. When one of the original parents is absent, the children need a special kind of understanding. An absent parent (who has died or who lives elsewhere and doesn't visit) is part of a child's past. The child must be allowed to have memories of this parent. The children who have access to both of their parents are those who adjust the best to divorce. They should be allowed to regularly speak with, visit, and write to their noncustodial parent.

Help the kids fit in. Children of stepfamilies belong to two households. It is understand-

able that they have questions about where they fit in. They are usually able to adjust to having two sets of rules as long as they are not asked to choose which is better.

Be clear about the rules. Ideally, both sets of parents should discuss the family rules and what will happen if rules are broken. When the adults agree on the rules, they should explain them to the children. Most successful stepfamilies have learned that the rules should be decided together in the beginning, and that the biological parent should do the explaining and disciplining. The stepparent may have more involvement after the relationships with the stepchildren have been established. All of this works best when the parents can agree to be flexible and cooperative with one another. This may be difficult immediately following a divorce or remarriage, but it is important to work toward this objective.

Educate yourselves and seek emotional support. Read books about managing stepfamilies, attend classes, and participate in stepfamily support groups. Seek the help of an experienced mental health professional to help you through the rough spots. Marriage and Family Therapists have specific skills and training for working with families and stepfamilies.

Give the kids their own space. Make physical space available for the children who don't live with you. Children need a sense of belonging. Creating a room or section of a room for visiting children will help them feel like part of your family.

Expect them to think it's temporary. Accept the fact that your children may expect you and their other parent to reconcile. They may fantasize that your new relationship with your partner is only temporary. This is especially true in the beginning. Find a time to sit down with the children and explain that when two people are unable to live together anymore, it doesn't mean they love their children any less. This is especially important for the parent who has moved away, since the children will inevitably feel a sense of rejection.

Expect resentment. No matter how good a parent you are, you will never be the biological parent of your stepchildren. It is natural for a stepchild to feel some resentment for you, especially when you are setting limits for their behavior.

Show the children love. Sometimes children need love the most at a time when it is the most difficult to give it to them. While bad behavior should never be rewarded, always praise children when they are behaving well.

Janet Asher is a licensed counselor and Clinical Director of the Family Therapy Center in Walnut Hills. Call 555-0987 for your free consultation.

Parenting Today

41. Parenting Your Teen with Less Stress

By Mark Cohen, M.A.

How to Maintain Communication

Even though teens need to separate from their parents during adolescence, they also need to know that the safety net of home and family is always there for them. If the lines of communication are shut down, they are not yet capable of surviving emotionally; they need support and input. Let's take a look at a few guidelines for keeping the lines of communication open between parents and teenagers.

1. Pay attention to the small things along with the significant things. If you are generally a good listener, your teen will be more likely to talk to you.
2. When your teen talks to you, pay attention. Don't be doing something else.
3. If you can't pay attention right at the moment, explain why. Ask if you can talk about the issue later, at a specific time.
4. Ask questions for clarification, but watch out for coming across as critical. If your teen sees your questions as disapproval, stop asking them.
5. Expect your teen to change his mind frequently. Avoid commenting on the inconsistencies.
6. Express interest and encouragement in your teen's activities.

7. Accept your teen's opinions, even if you don't agree with them.

Preventing High-Risk Behavior

All parents fear their teens becoming involved in high-risk behaviors such as drinking, smoking, and sexual activity. There are some very specific things you can do to minimize your teen's need to act out. Here are some tips for preventing high-risk behavior:

1. Be a part of your teen's life. If possible, be present when she is likely to be home.
2. Encourage your teen to talk to you openly at any time.
3. When your teen tells you things, watch your reaction. Avoid reactions that will cause him to think twice about being candid with you in the future.
4. Be specific about what kind of behavior you expect and what is unacceptable.
5. Keep harmful substances out of the house. This includes cigarettes, drugs, and alcohol. When teens have access to these items, they are more likely to use them.
6. Expect good things from your teen. Teens who know their parents expect the best have greater emotional well-being.
7. Encourage your teen to become involved in school activities. Those who are involved at school engage in fewer high-risk behaviors.

Preventing Teen Substance Abuse

Now let's talk about some of the risks that teens face. First, let's look at drugs and alcohol. These are a few things you can do to help your teen stay away from drugs and alcohol.

1. State your expectations clearly.
2. Pay attention to where your teen is.
3. When your teen leaves home, ask her to tell you where she is going. Ask for specifics.
4. If your teen says he is going one place but actually goes somewhere else, consider restricting his freedom for awhile.
5. Remember that your teen is innocent until proven guilty. Stay open to the possibility that there is a reasonable explanation for any story you might hear.
6. Build relationships with other parents and agree on the rules. If none of the kids in the group have complete freedom, there will be less peer pressure and more safety.

Teen Depression

Teens are known for their mood swings. It is common for them to feel sad or gloomy. Many parents become concerned about a teen's moods.

Depression is different from the blues because it lasts longer and is more intense. Clinical depression is an illness that can lead to very serious problems, with lifelong implications. Some of the warning signs that your teen may have something more serious than the blues are:

1. She shows less interest in her appearance.
2. She seems to feel hopeless.

3. He seems to hate himself.
4. He seems indifferent about most things.
5. She seems numb.
6. She lacks energy.
7. He talks or thinks about death and dying.
8. He changes his sleeping or eating habits.
9. She loses interest in her friends or hobbies.
10. She stops caring about her pets or cherished possessions.
11. He has a sudden change in his grades at school.
12. He complains of extraordinary stress.
13. She withdraws from people.

If you think your teen's mood may be depression, here are some things you can do about it:

1. Talk to your teen about how he is feeling. Help him get it off his chest. Encourage him to think of solutions to what is bothering him.
2. Encourage your teen to participate in some kind of physical activity.
3. Check in with her more often than usual.
4. If these steps don't help and the problem seems serious, call a school counselor, teacher, or doctor. Ask for a referral to a qualified, licensed professional who specializes in working with adolescents who have emotional problems.

Eating Disorders

Eating disorders affect more girls than boys during adolescence. They are emotional disorders that require the intervention of a health professional before they become life-threatening. If you think your teen suffers from either anorexia or bulimia, do not hesitate to seek the advice of your physician. Early treatment greatly enhances the chances of recovery.

These are the warning signs for **anorexia:**

1. She has lost 25% of normal body weight without being on a diet.
2. She has a distorted body image.
3. She diets constantly even though she is thin.
4. She fears gaining weight.
5. Her menstrual periods have stopped (this is known as amenorrhea).
6. She is preoccupied with food, calories, and eating.
7. She exercises excessively.
8. She binges and purges.

The warning signs for **bulimia** include the following:

1. She eats uncontrollably (binges), often in secret.
2. She purges by vomiting, abusing laxatives or diuretics, or vigorously exercising. She may also compensate for eating with strict dieting or fasting.
3. She frequently visits the bathroom after eating a meal.
4. She is preoccupied with her body weight.
5. She experiences depression or mood swings.
6. She has irregular periods.
7. She has dental problems, swollen cheek glands, or is bloated.

If you think your teen suffers from either anorexia or bulimia, do not hesitate to seek the advice of your physician. Early treatment greatly enhances the chances of recovery.

How to Build Your Teen's Self-Esteem

Having strong self-esteem is critical, especially during the teen years. This is true for the following reasons:

- Self-esteem is a significant factor in how each of us manages our life.
- How we feel about ourselves guides the choices we make, how we feel, how we respond to events, and just about everything else we do.
- Strong self-esteem enables us to make constructive choices for ourselves and others.
- When our self-esteem is weak, we tend to make choices based on what others think and want, rather than on what is really best for us.

You can help your teen build and maintain his or her self-esteem in the following ways:

1. Listen to what your teen is saying to you, in words and actions.
2. Ask your teen's opinion about things and accept it.
3. Ask why he thinks the way he does.
4. Remind yourself that your teen needs to differentiate herself from you. That is her job as an adolescent, and it is healthy. Allow her to do it.
5. Let him know that you love him.
6. Let her know that you will always be there for her.
7. Give him permission to explore ideas.
8. Don't be threatened when she expresses herself.
9. Encourage him to express his feelings appropriately.

Please pass this newsletter along to a friend. Or call 555-0987 to request additional copies.

Mark Cohen is a licensed counselor in Pasadena. He specializes in working with adolescents and their families. He offers several groups and classes on a regular basis, both for parents and teens. Call 555-0987 for your free consultation.

Suggested Reading

Louise Bates Ames, Frances L. Ilg and Sidney M. Baker, *Your Ten- to Fourteen-Year-Old*. New York: Dell Trade Paperbacks, 1988.

Ruth Bell, *Changing Bodies, Changing Selves, 3rd Edition*. New York, NY: Times Books, 1998.

Kate Kelly, *The Complete Idiot's Guide to Parenting a Teenager*. New York, NY: Alpha Books, 1996.

Wade Horn and Carol Keough, *Better Homes & Gardens New Teen Book*. Des Moines, IA: Meredith Books, 1999.

Michael Riera, *Uncommon Sense for Parents with Teenagers*. Berkeley, CA: Celestial Arts, 1995.

Marriage Report

42. Recovering from an Affair

By Susan Lee, Ph.D.

Infidelity is more common than most people realize. In fact, it is estimated that 60% of men and 40% of women today will have an extramarital affair during their marriage. I decided to learn as much as I could about it so I could help my clients prevent it, or recover from it when it has already happened. In this newsletter, I will explore the forces that lead to infidelity and what must happen for couples to heal.

Forms of Infidelity

Infidelity takes many forms. Some people have *sequential affairs*—a series of one-night stands or short affairs. These affairs involve very little emotional investment and may be rationalized as harmless. There is always the danger of contracting a sexually transmitted disease. When such behavior continues for several years and finally is discovered, it is difficult to heal the years of deceit.

Other affairs are *discrete events*. These also involve minimal emotional investment.

Sometimes affairs last longer and become more serious. These affairs may be quite romantic and sexual. Sometimes they grow into more *serious relationships* and may last for years.

Why Affairs Happen

Infidelity happens for many reasons. Here are a few of the common explanations:

1. An affair may be a response to a crisis such as the death of someone important, moving to a new city, a job change, or some other kind of life transition.
2. Sometimes people become bored with their partners and seek sexual or emotional excitement with someone new. The new person seems to supply the excitement that has been missing.
3. Stressful times in the family life cycle lead some to seek escape in an affair. This includes things like taking care of aging parents, raising teenagers, and becoming new parents.
4. People sometimes look for outside relationships because their expectations of marriage have not been satisfied.
5. Some people seek outside relationships when their partners are emotionally unavailable because of illness.
6. Other people begin affairs because they seek more affection than their partner can provide.
7. Other people seek professional or social advancement.

There are also many social reasons why affairs happen: factors that exist in our society that lead many of us to expect a fantasy version of marriage that could never really exist. When marriage doesn't live up to this expectation, some of us keep looking for it outside of marriage.

Signs of Infidelity

The following signs indicate that your partner may be unfaithful. These are things that people have noticed before discovering that their partners were having affairs. None of the items by themselves mean that infidelity is about to happen, but they may be cause for concern if they are part of a larger pattern that is causing concern. These may apply to either men or women partners.

1. He has recently lost weight.
2. She has changed her hair color or hairstyle.
3. He begins wearing a different style of underwear.
4. She pays more attention to her clothing and appearance than she did in the past.
5. He begins using a different brand of soap or shampoo.
6. She uses breath mints, when she didn't use them in the past.
7. He stops wearing his wedding ring.
8. She wears more jewelry than she used to.
9. He buys a sports car.
10. She changes the position of the passenger car seat.
11. One number is repeated on the cellular phone bill.
12. He doesn't leave a number where he can be reached.
13. She gives vague answers about where she will be.
14. He has sudden work obligations that keep him from attending family events.
15. She begins attending more conferences.
16. He has more business dinners than he used to.
17. She has an extra key on her key ring.
18. He has restaurant matchbooks in his pocket.
19. There is lipstick or makeup on his shirt.
20. She often makes excuses to go out alone.
21. He goes for more workouts at the gym.
22. She smells like she just took a shower.
23. He seems emotionally distant or preoccupied.
24. She seems less interested in family activities.
25. He changes his sexual behavior, wanting either more or less.
26. You have a gut feeling that something is wrong.

Common Reactions to Infidelity

People who are involved in relationships in which their partner has been unfaithful say they have a wide range of reactions. These are a few of the common ones:

1. A physical reaction, such as feeling like you have been punched in the stomach.
2. Denying that anything is wrong.
3. Blaming yourself (I didn't pay enough attention to her; I wasn't sexy enough for him; I let myself get too fat, etc.).
4. Blaming your partner (I can't believe anything she says)
5. Blaming the relationship (We were too young; We were wrong for each other; We had different values, etc.).
6. Blaming the lover (It's all his fault; If it weren't for him); transferring anger from one's spouse to one's lover.

Other Consequences of Infidelity

In addition to the emotional impact of infidelity, there may also be other consequences: sexually transmitted diseases, pregnancy, problems at work, and loss of relationships.

Recovery Strategies

Even though infidelity has a devastating impact on marriages, many do survive. Let's look at what it takes for a relationship to recover.

If You Were Unfaithful

If *you* had the affair and want to save your marriage:

1. Stop the affair and tell the truth about it.
2. Make the choice to practice fidelity.
3. Understand your partner's need to ask questions and understand what happened.
4. Spend plenty of time with your family.
5. Find a therapist and explore what has happened in your marriage.
6. Expect to reassure your partner of your commitment to the marriage.
7. Listen carefully to your partner and accept his or her feelings and thoughts.
8. Admit that you were wrong. Write a letter to your partner and admit everything. Let it all out.
9. Make amends. Identify what it would take for you to deserve forgiveness. Then, do it.

If Your Partner Was Unfaithful

If *your partner* had the affair and *you* want to save your marriage:

1. Acknowledge your anger and express it productively.
2. Be aware of distorted thoughts that may fuel your anger.
3. Watch out for negative beliefs that may make it harder for you to heal your relationship.
4. Find a way to explore and express your feelings, such as writing in a journal or working with a professional therapist.
5. Explore the advantages and disadvantages of saving your marriage.
6. Establish a safe environment where you can learn about what happened.
7. When you are ready, create a ritual for letting go of the anger and forgiving.

Prevention Steps

Finally, what are some things you can do to protect your marriage and keep it from becoming an infidelity statistic?

1. Pay attention to your partner. Be aware of his or her needs and do your best to meet them.
2. Think about how you behaved when you were trying to win your partner over. Do the same things now.
3. Make sex fun.
4. Look for opportunities to talk and listen.
5. Be thoughtful and romantic. Send cards, flowers, gifts.
6. Avoid high-risk situations. Discuss these with your partner and ask him or her to do the same.
7. Be polite to your partner.
8. Say nice things about your partner, in public and in private.
9. Spend regular private time together.
10. Greet your partner when he or she comes home.
11. Show that you are glad to see your partner. Be energized and pleasant.
12. Recommit to your values. Make the decision to live in keeping with what you believe is right.
13. Accept that you are responsible for your own well-being.

135

14. Be proactive about nurturing your marriage. This relationship is your most important investment; give it the time and attention it deserves.
15. Look for ways to express appreciation and respect.
16. Think of ways to enhance your partner's self-esteem.

Susan Lee is a licensed counselor in Elmhurst. She specializes in working with couples and families, and offers ongoing groups for individuals and couples. Call 555-0987 for your free consultation.

Suggested Reading

Pittman, Frank, *Private Lies: Infidelity and the Betrayal of Intimacy*. New York, NY: W.W. Norton & Company, 1989.

Staheli, Lana, *Affair-Proof Your Marriage: Understanding, Preventing and Surviving An Affair*. New York, NY: HarperCollins, 1995.

Subotnik, Rona and Harris, Gloria, *Surviving Infidelity: Making Decisions, Recovering from the Pain*. Holbrook, MA: Adams Publishing, 1994.

Vaughan, Peggy, *The Monogamy Myth*. New York, NY: Newmarket Press, 1989.

Better Relationships

43. Resolving Conflicts in Relationships

By Samantha Shea, M.A.

Every relationship has conflicts. In some relationships, conflict is a serious problem; in others, differences seem to be resolved without creating a major incident.

Think about the kinds of conflicts that happen in your daily life. These are typical:

1. Disagreements over who should do what
2. Disagreements over how things should be done
3. Conflicts of personality and style

Nonproductive Ways of Dealing with Conflict

Now that we've identified some typical situations where conflict arises in your everyday lives, let's look at some examples of ways that people deal with them. These are the common ones:

1. Avoid the conflict.
2. Deny the conflict; wait until it goes away.
3. Change the subject.
4. React emotionally: Become aggressive, abusive, hysterical, or frightening.
5. Find someone to blame.

6. Make excuses.
7. Let someone else deal with it.

All of these responses to conflict have one thing in common: They are all nonproductive. All of them are destructive, some physically. This is why learning to manage conflict is so important.

Factors That Affect How People Manage Conflict

The skills involved in managing conflict are learned behaviors. None of us is born knowing how to deal with differences of opinion, arguments, or turf wars. Some of the factors that affect how we behave in the face of conflict are:

1. **Behavior learned in families.** In some families, conflict and confrontation are a communication style. In others, conflict always remains hidden.

2. **Behavior learned from role models.** People who have had a teacher or boss who modeled effective conflict resolution skills are more likely to develop these skills themselves.

3. **Status.** People in higher-status positions usually feel freer to engage in conflict and are less likely to avoid confrontation.

4. **Unwritten rules.** Some groups encourage conflict; others have unwritten rules that it is to be contained or avoided.

5. **Gender differences.** Males are generally encouraged to be more confrontational than females.

Active Listening

Active listening is a valuable skill for resolving conflicts because it enables you to demonstrate that you understand what another person is saying and how he or she is feeling about it. Active listening means restating, in your own words, what the other person has said.

Active listening is a way of checking whether your understanding is correct. It also demonstrates that you are listening and that you are interested and concerned. These all help resolve a situation where there are conflicting points of view.

Active listening responses have two components: (1) naming the feeling that the other person is conveying, and (2) stating the reason for the feeling.

Here are some examples of active-listening statements:

"Sounds like you're upset about what happened at work."
"You're annoyed by my lateness, aren't you?"
"You sound really stumped about how to solve this problem."
"It makes you angry when you find errors on Joe's paperwork."
"Sounds like you're really worried about Wendy."
"I get the feeling you're awfully busy right now."

Actively listening is *not* the same as agreement. It is a way of demonstrating that you intend to hear and understand another's point of view.

Benefits of Active Listening

If a person uses active listening as part of his or her communication style, it has a positive effect on dealing with conflicts when they arise. This is because of the following benefits:

1. It feels good when another person makes an effort to understand what you are thinking and feeling. It creates good feelings about the other person and makes you feel better about yourself.
2. Restating what you've heard and checking for understanding promotes better communication and produces fewer misunderstandings.
3. Responding with active listening has a calming effect in an emotional situation.

General Tips for Managing Conflict

1. Stick with "I" statements; avoid "you" statements.
2. Avoid name-calling and put-downs ("A reasonable person could see that . . .").
3. Soften your tone.
4. Take a time-out ("Let's take a break and cool down").
5. Acknowledge the other person's point of view (agreement is not necessary).
6. Avoid defensive or hostile body language (rolling eyes, crossing arms in front of body, tapping foot).
7. Be specific and factual; avoid generalities.

Preventing Conflicts

Now that we've talked about how to resolve a conflict, let's look at how to prevent conflicts from happening. Think of situations in your life where there don't seem to be many conflicts. What might be happening there? Chances are, you are practicing one of the following conflict-prevention skills:

1. Bring issues out in the open before they become problems.

2. Be aware of triggers and respond to them when you notice them.

3. Have a process for resolving conflicts. Discuss the process with those around you and get agreement on what people should do in cases of differing viewpoints.

Samantha Shea is a licensed Professional Counselor in Sioux City. She specializes in working with couples and families. Call 555-0987 for your free consultation.

A Successful Life

44. Should You Leave Your Relationship?

By Sandra Yee, M.A.

 How do you know when it's time to say goodbye to a relationship? In any intimate relationship— especially in a marriage—it's not a good idea to let a doomed partnership drag on, simply to avoid the pain of a breakup.

Signs of Trouble

There are some warning signs that your relationship is in trouble. If you recognize any of these signals in your own partnership, you may have some work to do to get things back on track.

1. **Your life priorities have changed significantly.** Major life changes often force people to reconsider what's important, and this can make a once-healthy partnership lose its bearings. A near-death experience such as a serious accident or illness, being unexpectedly fired from a job, or losing a family member can cause anyone to reevaluate his or her life and decide to make some changes. Everything looks different after such an experience, and some things lose their meaning. When this happens, these new ways of seeing things must be addressed, since it's unlikely that such changes will just disappear.

2. **The arrangement still works, but the passion is missing.** Lots of doomed relationships manage to work—for a while. But when neither partner has any genuine enthusiasm for the relationship, it may be in trouble.

3. **You no longer trust your partner.** After a partner has broken the bond of trust, it can be difficult to get it back. If your partner has had an affair or was irresponsible with a large amount of money, it is understandable that you feel angry and hurt. Over time, these wounds may not heal. Broken trust can cause serious harm to a relationship, and, if it is not healed, the relationship may not recover.

4. **Your partner's lifestyle or values clash with yours.** It is difficult to sustain a long-term relationship when you and your partner do not agree on some of life's most basic things. If you want to make and save a lot of money, but your partner seeks a simple life and would be happy living in a small house with few luxuries, this is a potential problem. If your partner seeks excitement and wants to be around people most of the time but you are basically a loner who prefers solitude, you may find yourselves growing apart. You may have

been attracted to each other in the beginning because you brought each other some balance, but, over the long term, the very things that drew you to each other may doom your relationship.

Deciding to end a relationship can have enormous implications. If you are married, have children, own a home, and share finances, leaving your partner can be very complicated and will affect everyone in the family. It is important to make such a decision thoughtfully and for the right reasons.

More Warning Signs

If your partner regularly does one or more of the following things, you have good reason to be concerned.

1. Behaves abusively with your friends and family
2. Betrays your trust
3. Breaks promises
4. Cheats on you
5. Does not challenge you mentally
6. Does not support your goals in life
7. Is extremely jealous without cause
8. Is not financially self-supporting
9. Opposes or ignores your thoughts, feelings, or concerns
10. Physically abuses you
11. Pressures you to have sex when you are not interested
12. Resists your attempts to improve the relationship
13. Shares your secrets with others
14. Tells lies regularly
15. Threatens violence
16. Tries to isolate you from your friends and family
17. Verbally abuses you or puts you down

These behaviors are very serious and potentially dangerous to you. If you are in a relationship with someone who treats you in any of these ways, you should seriously consider seeking the assistance of a mental health professional.

The Impact of Stress

Stress can make it harder to decide what to do. If you are questioning your relationship and have problems with money, are stressed at work, or the kids are acting up, deciding what to do becomes even more difficult. It's important to take your time and resist the temptation to make a fast decision that may later turn out to be the wrong thing for you.

Tips for Making Good Relationship Decisions

1. Take your time making any important decision such as whether to end an important relationship. Even though you may feel confused and indecisive, it is important to recognize that this situation requires a deliberate and careful decision-making process.
2. Making a relationship decision calls for *both* instinct and logic. It's important to trust your gut, but don't lose track of reason.
3. Look at the issues from different points of view.
4. Consider the immediate and long-term implications of each option (staying or

leaving), including the impact of each on other people in your life.

5. Consider the worst- and best-case scenarios, as well as the possibilities in between.

6. Give your relationship every chance to get back on track before you call it quits. Ask yourself if you have really tried everything. If you have, and it still isn't working, it may be time to move on.

Seeking Advice and Support

Involving a few trusted friends in your decision-making process can help you avoid the tendency to rush into a decision and hurry to get it over with. Consulting others helps you step back from the situation and see it in a broader context. While it is more difficult and time-consuming, getting the advice and support of others can help you reach a better decision about whether to end the relationship. This is true for relationships or any other kind of decision.

You may decide to work with a professional counselor or therapist during this process. *This is strongly advised if you are in an abusive relationship.* A licensed, experienced professional can help you sort out the issues, help you see things you may not be aware of, and give you feedback on how you are seeing things. Involving an objective outsider can be a smart move because you can feel free to say everything that is on your mind without worrying about offending someone you care about or being judged for your thoughts and feelings.

Finally, if you decide that the relationship should end, minimize the chances for emotional fallout by planning how, where, and when you will deliver the news. When making such an important change in your life, it is better to set aside spontaneity in favor of being slow, deliberate, and certain.

Suggested Reading

Hammond, John, Keeney, Ralph and Raiffa, Howard, *Smart Choices: A Practical Guide to Making Better Decisions.* Harvard Business School Press, 1998.

Heller, Robert and Hindle, Tim, *Essential Manager's Manual.* New York, NY: DK Publishing, 1998.

Sandra Yee is a licensed counselor in St. Charles. She specializes in working with adults who are experiencing separation and divorce. Call 555-0987 for your free consultation.

Marriage Today

45. Skills for Making Your Marriage Thrive

By Wendy Williams, Ph.D.

Any marriage counselor will tell you that one of the most common problems observed when couples come for help is poor communication skills. People get into trouble in their marriages because they have not developed their ability to listen and communicate.

Barriers to Communication

These are a few of the things that prevent people from communicating effectively:

- Not knowing how to communicate properly
- Not taking the time to think through what you want to say
- Not taking the time to anticipate what your partner might be thinking and feeling
- Fear of revealing too much of yourself
- Fear of your partner's anger
- Not wanting to hurt your partner's feelings

Empathy and Acceptance

People marry because they want to spend the rest of their lives with their partner. They have every hope of growing together and creating a relationship that makes them feel emotionally healthy. Two factors that are necessary for this to happen are empathy and acceptance on the part of both partners.

Empathy is the capacity to put oneself in another's shoes and understand how they view their reality, how they feel about things.

Demonstrating empathy and acceptance is critical to maintaining a strong relationship. Let's look next at some communication skills that enable you to create a climate of empathy, acceptance, and understanding. First we will explore a skill called Active Listening.

Active Listening

Active listening is a way of communicating that creates the important climate of empathy, acceptance, and understanding.

- It is a two-step response to a statement made by your partner.
- It includes reflecting back what emotion you detected in the statement, and the reason for the emotion.

This is what active listening sounds like:

"Sounds like you're upset about what happened at work."
"You're very annoyed by my lateness, aren't you?"

Why Active Listening Is a Valuable Skill

Active listening is a valuable skill because it demonstrates that you understand what your partner is saying and how he or she is feeling about it.

- Active listening means restating, in your own words, what the other person has said.
- It's a check on whether your understanding is correct.
- It demonstrates that you are listening and that you are interested and concerned.

Actively listening does *not* mean agreeing with the other person. The point is to demonstrate to your partner that you intend to hear and understand his or her point of view. This is good for your relationship for several reasons:

- When someone demonstrates that they want to understand what you are thinking and feeling, it feels good.
- It creates good feelings about the other person.
- Restating and checking understanding promotes better communication and fewer misunderstandings.

More Active Listening Examples

Here are some more examples of active listening:

"You sound really stumped about how to solve this problem."
"It makes you angry when you find errors on Joey's homework."
"Sounds like you're really worried about Wendy."
"I get the feeling you're awfully busy right now."

More Communication Skills

Although our space is limited in this short newsletter, there are a few more communication skills that I must mention. These include asking open-ended questions, making sum-

mary statements to check understanding, and encouraging your partner to open up and elaborate by using neutral questions and phrases.

Open-ended questions begin with *what, why, how do,* or *tell me.*

- These questions get the other person to open up and elaborate on the topic.
- Asking these kinds of questions gets the other person involved by giving him or her a chance to tell what he or she thinks or knows.
- These questions are designed to encourage your partner to talk.
- They are useful when the other person is silent or reluctant to elaborate.
- They are also useful in dealing with negative emotions (such as anger or fear), since they help encourage the other person to vent feelings.

Summary Statements

Summary statements sum up what you hear your partner saying.

- A summary statement enhances your partner's self-esteem by showing that you were listening carefully.
- It also helps you focus on facts, not emotions.
- It helps your partner clarify his or her own thinking by hearing your summary.
- Summary statements also help you deal with multiple disagreements so you can deal with them one by one.
- They help eliminate confusion by focusing on the relevant facts.
- Summary statements also help you separate the important issues from the trivial.

Neutral Questions and Phrases

Neutral questions and phrases get your partner to open up and elaborate on the topic you are discussing.

- These questions are more focused than open-ended questions.
- They help your partner understand what you are interested in hearing more about.
- They further communication because they help you gain more information.
- When you ask these kinds of questions, you demonstrate to your partner that you are interested and that you are listening.

Business Skills for Marriages

You might be surprised to hear that the same skills that help people succeed in business can also be used to build a better marriage. Like any business, a marriage is a partnership of people. Many of the skills that make businesses run successfully—planning, organizing, and setting goals—also can be applied to running your marriage successfully. These are some of the skills that will strengthen any marriage:

1. Create an overall vision of what you want your life to be like; consider all life areas.
2. Develop a long-range strategy.
3. Set short-term and long-term goals.
4. Plan the steps that will help you accomplish your goals.
5. Organize projects.
6. Manage projects.
7. Manage people.
8. Evaluate progress and results at regular intervals.
9. Revise goals as needed.

Please pass this newsletter along to a friend. Or call 555-0987 to request additional copies.

Suggested Reading

Alberti and Emmons, *Your Perfect Right.* San Luis Obispo, CA: Impact Publishers, 1970.

Burley-Allen, Madelyn, *Managing Assertively: A Self-Teaching Guide* (2nd Edition). New York, NY: John Wiley & Sons, 1995.

Burley-Allen, Madelyn, *Listening: The Forgotten Skill* (2nd Edition). New York, NY: John Wiley & Sons, 1995.

Gordon, Thomas, *Leader Effectiveness Training.* New York: Bantam Doubleday Dell, 1986.

McKay, Matthew, Rogers, Peter and McKay, Judith. *When Anger Hurts: Quieting the Storm Within.* Oakland, CA: New Harbinger Publications, 1989.

Rosellini, Gayle and Worden, Mark, *Of Course You're Angry* (Second Edition). Center City, MN: Hazelden Foundation, 1997.

Staheli, Lana, *Affair-Proof Your Marriage: Understanding, Preventing and Surviving an Affair.* New York, NY: HarperCollins, 1995.

Tavris, Carol, *Anger: The Misunderstood Emotion.* New York: Touchstone, 1989.

Wendy Williams is a licensed Marriage and Family Therapist in Greater Barrington. She is the Clinical Director of The Barrington Marriage Clinic. Call 555-0987 for your free consultation.

Parenting News

46. Single-Parent Survival Skills

By Lucy Goldberg, Ph.D.

Emotional Overload

Many single parents say they deal with a variety of emotional issues that you might describe as "extra baggage." Some examples include:

- Self-pity
- Depression
- Guilt
- Anger
- Envy
- Fear
- Severe money problems
- Loneliness and isolation
- Frustration
- Exhaustion

These issues present such a challenge because they undermine your daily functioning and emotional well-being. But they *can* be managed successfully so that you manage your family in a positive way.

10 Ways to Speed Your Recovery Process

Becoming divorced or widowed and then facing years of single parenting is a shock to anyone who experiences it. You will need to take steps to recover and heal. Here are some suggestions:

1. Some churches, synagogues, counseling centers, and therapists offer free and low-cost divorce recovery workshops and grief support groups. Look for them in the newspaper and Yellow Pages. If you don't see any listed, call a few places that may be able to refer you.
2. Look for local peer support groups and networks.
3. If you have access to the Internet, search for support services in your area.
4. Also on the Internet, look for chat rooms or bulletin boards where single parents post messages and share ideas.
5. Find library books for kids about divorce and single-parent families, and read them together. Take the time to talk about how they relate to your situation and encourage your kids to talk about their feelings.
6. Find a support group for children of divorce.
7. Tell your children's teachers and the school psychologist that you are a single-parent family. Let them know that you welcome feedback and suggestions on coping with your circumstances.
8. When you are ready, investigate groups like Parents Without Partners for single adults. You need to be with other adults who have similar interests.
9. Learn to help your kids talk about what is happening to them.
10. Learn conflict resolution and problem-solving skills.

Single-Parent Survival Strategies

In addition to recovering from the loss of a partner, you will need to take action to survive and thrive in the coming years. The following strategies provide a starting place.

1. Watch out for too many changes in your life as you recover from both the loss of your spouse and the resulting changes in your life circumstances. Change causes stress, and you have enough right now.
2. Realize and accept that you must get help with your single-parenting responsibilities. It is unrealistic to think that you can do it alone.
3. Manage your own emotions so you will be able to help your child manage his or her struggle. Learn as much as you can about how children respond to divorce, the death of a parent, or life in a single-parent home. Do not expect your child to respond the same way you do. Take your child's developmental stage into consideration when responding to his or her behavior.
4. Give your children permission to talk to you about their feelings.
5. Keep appropriate boundaries.
   - Don't give in to the temptation to let your child take care of you.
   - Let your children be children.
   - Avoid burdening them with your feelings and the facts of the divorce or death of your spouse.
   - Find another adult to be your sounding board.
6. Let people help you.
   - If it is impossible to reciprocate, say so.
   - People know that your life isn't like it used to be.
   - Don't let your inability to reciprocate prevent you from accepting what people willingly offer.
7. Let go of your need for perfection. You will have much more stress if you don't lower your expectations.
8. Even though you are unable to be present as much as in the past, your children still need adult supervision. Look for ways for other adults to look in on your kids when they are home alone, even when they are teenagers.
9. Just because your child appears to be handling his or her emotions well, don't assume that he or she is okay. Some kids respond to parent loss by becoming overly responsible or by closing down their emotions. They may need to hear, "Tell me how you're feeling."
10. While it is important to listen and accept your children's feelings, it is equally important to set limits on behavior.
11. Cultivate your ability to be flexible and find creative ways to solve problems.
12. Learn to set priorities. Do the most important things first.
13. Trust your gut feelings. Pay attention to your instincts and act on them.
14. Simplify as many things as possible in your life. You cannot afford to keep it complicated.
15. Find an outlet for your anger. If a friend is not available, look for a minister, rabbi, or professional counselor. If money is an issue, look for a therapist who will see you for a low fee.
16. Teach yourself to let go of guilt. You don't have time for it, and it's not necessary.
17. Focus on issues you have control over. If something is beyond your control, don't waste your emotions on it.

18. Create a ritual to mark the change in your circumstances. This could be a funeral for your spouse or a ceremony to acknowledge your divorce.

19. Keep a private journal in which you express your feelings. Be sure to keep it in a private place where your children won't find it. A journal provides a place to express anger, sadness, loneliness, and fear—all of those feelings you feel every day as a single parent.

20. Remind yourself that recovering from divorce or the death of a spouse will take time. Your recovery will happen on its own schedule, and it will happen. You will get through this intact.

21. Learn to be assertive. You can't say yes to every request, whether it is from your family members or people in the community who want your time and resources. If you give it all away, you will have nothing left for yourself.

22. Find ways to take care of your body. Get regular checkups and make time to exercise. You need rest now more than ever. Watch your alcohol intake.

23. Find someone who will listen to you. Sometimes you have to ask, for example, "I need a sounding board right now. Can I have 15 minutes of your time?"

24. Rent a sad movie and let yourself cry (when the kids aren't around). Crying allows you to release the sadness that you are sure to feel.

25. Do at least one fun thing for yourself every week.

26. In your private journal, make a list of all the things you're afraid of.

27. In your private journal, make a list of all the things you worry about.

28. Get together with other single-parent families. Sharing times with people facing similar issues can make you feel normal.

Please pass this newsletter along to a friend. Or call 555-0987 to request additional copies.

Suggested Reading

R. Alberti and M. Emmons, *Your Perfect Right.* San Luis Obispo, CA: Impact Publishers, 1970.

Louise Bates Ames, Frances L. Ilg and Sidney M. Baker, *Your Ten- to Fourteen-Year-Old.* New York: Dell Trade Paperbacks, 1988. (This book is part of the Gesell series, which includes *Your One-Year-Old, Your Two-Year-Old, Your Three-Year-Old, Your Four-Year-Old, Your Five-Year-Old, Your Six-Year-Old, Your Seven-Year-Old, Your Eight-Year-Old,* and *Your Nine-Year-Old.*

S. Bower and G. Bower, *Asserting Your Self.* Reading, MA: Addison-Wesley Publishing Co., Inc., 1976.

Linda Foust, *The Single Parent's Almanac.* Rocklin, CA: Prima Publishing, 1996.

Gary Richmond, *Successful Single Parenting: Going It Alone.* Eugene, OR: Harvest House Publishers, 1990.

Lucy Goldberg is a licensed psychologist in Farnsworth. She specializes in working with both parents and children, and offers a variety of parenting classes and support groups. She is also the author of "Single Parent Challenges." Call 555-0987 for your free consultation and class schedule.

The Family Therapy Newsletter

47. How to Manage Sibling Rivalry

By Jane Nordstrom, M.S.

It is human nature to feel competitive and envious toward others. A moderate spirit of competition is a positive and productive attribute in school and in business. Sibling rivalry is a normal part of growing up in families. The competition between siblings starts when the second child is born. Unfortunately, many parents ignore it and some even make the situation worse.

When occasional fighting becomes a constant series of arguments and fights, it must be dealt with to avoid years of discord and even potential danger. Here are some tips that will help you lessen your frustration over argumentative brothers and sisters and help them learn to get along better.

Do your best to offer each of your children equal amounts of praise and attention. This is true if they are competing for your attention or if they are participating in a school or sports activity.

Encourage your children to participate in activities that they truly enjoy. Don't expect them to always join activities that they must do together or where they will be competing against each other.

Children sometimes perceive that their parents favor one child over the others. While some parents do prefer one child to the others, it is usually not a conscious choice. If your child tells you that you favor his or her sibling, pay attention to your behavior; maybe there is some truth to it. However, if you know you are being fair or if there is a valid reason for treating one child differently, stand firm. Sometimes children use the "favorite child" complaint as a way to make you feel guilty and give them what they want.

Sometimes one child is more cooperative or better behaved than another. It's normal to compare siblings, but it's generally better not to talk about it. Comparing two kids doesn't help improve their behavior; instead, it intensifies the sense of envy and jealousy. A more constructive strategy is to limit your comments to the problem behavior. Always avoid telling one child that his or her sibling does something better.

Make it a rule that family members may become involved in incidents between siblings only if they actually saw what happened. This keeps people from being manipulated.

Realize that younger children can be the aggressors. Don't automatically rush to their defense.

If two kids are fighting over a toy, take it away. This discourages them from arguing over who can play with what.

When two kids are fighting, make them share a chair and look at each other in a mirror. With all the goofy faces they make in the mirror the disagreement is soon forgotten and they are laughing like best friends.

If the kids continue the fight after a few minutes in the chair, assign them a chore to do.

The excess energy they are directing toward each other is soon put to better use setting the table or picking up the toys.

Use the Active Listening technique to allow siblings to express their feelings. When kids fight, parents often try to talk children out of their feelings by saying things like "Stop arguing with Tony, Sarah. You know you love your brother." Instead, you could acknowledge the child's feelings by saying, "Sounds like you're pretty upset with Tony." You might be surprised to see that this defuses the emotion and enables Tony to move on to something else.

When you give things to children, base your choices on their individual needs and interests. If you try to avoid arguments by giving equal gifts to each child, they will inevitably find something about them that is unfair.

When your children are in an argument, avoid taking sides. If you can, encourage them to work out their differences. It is almost impossible to try to determine who started a fight. Even if you know who started the argument, taking sides only makes things worse. If your children learn that you will not enter their minor disagreements, they will have to learn to settle things between themselves.

Take a parent education instructor course. As you educate yourself about parenting, you will change some of your attitudes toward your children and learn new ways to interact with them. You can have the kind of family you want if you are willing to work at it, make some changes in your own behavior, and be patient for things to improve.

tence, your children will learn how to get along better. That will prepare them to have productive relationships in the future.

Please pass this newsletter along to a friend. Or call 555-0987 to request additional copies.

You may think that rivalry will stop magically if only you learn to do the right thing. However, learning new behaviors takes a lot of time and persistence.

It is important to address the issues of sibling rivalry when children are young, because it can intensify and persist as children become adults. It is important not to give up when you feel frustrated. Things may even seem like they are worse before they start to improve. Because of your efforts and persis-

Jane Nordstrom is a licensed counselor and Clinical Director of the Parents' Resource Center in South Barrington. Call 555-0987 for your free consultation.

News for Healthy Families

48. How to Help Your Child Have Strong Self-Esteem

By Amy Morita, MSW

Here is a list of ways to convey the message "You are worthwhile" to your children. This list could fill a hundred newsletters, since the ways to raise responsible, happy children are limited only by our imaginations. Here are some places to begin.

1. Tell her on a regular basis that you love her. Actually say the words. If you think, "I don't have to tell her. She knows," you are wrong. It doesn't count if you think it but don't say it out loud.

2. Tell him that you are glad he is your child. Say the words and mean them. If you don't feel it, there is something wrong and you should find out what's going on. We all have moments when we have a hard time getting in touch with our positive feelings for our children. I'm not talking about those times. I'm talking about in general, most of the time, if you're not feeling good about being your child's parent, something is wrong. He will never feel good about himself if he senses that you are not connected to him.

3. Give her an example to follow. Take the time to teach her the steps. Kids need models. It's unfair to expect that she will know what to do in her daily life if you haven't shown her how to do it.

4. Spend time with him. If you are absent most of the time, he notices, and he probably thinks it's because he isn't important enough.

5. Look at her when you speak to her. This conveys, "This is important and you are important."

6. Look at him when he speaks to you. This conveys, "What you are saying is important. You are important."

7. Explain why. It takes more time, but it conveys that she is important enough to spend the time helping her understand. When you explain why, you are also saying, "I understand that you need to know why. I am going to help you meet your needs."

8. When he tells you about something that happened, ask him how he feels about it. Take the time to listen to his answer.

9. When you ask a question, encourage her to elaborate. Say, "Tell me more about that," or ask, "What was that like?"

10. When you ask a question, don't interrupt when she is answering.

11. When you ask a question, watch your responses. Don't disagree or criticize his answer. This teaches him that it isn't safe to be candid and will make him edit what he tells you.

12. Take her seriously.

13. Participate in the driving. The kids whose parents never help with the driving feel bad about themselves.

14. Say no when you need to say no. Kids need to know there are limits and that some things are outside of those limits.

15. When you say no, explain why.

16. When you say yes, explain why.

17. Set a positive example with your own behavior. You can only expect her to behave with dignity and self-respect if she sees you doing it.

18. When you lose your temper or make a mistake, apologize. Say that you are sorry, be specific about what you are sorry for, and give him a chance to respond.

19. When you know that you have disappointed him, acknowledge it. Ask him how he feels about it.

20. Spend time alone with her. Arrange activities for just the two of you.

21. Ask him what *he* would like to do.

22. Give her a private space where she can express herself.

23. Respect his privacy.

24. If he did a good job on something, say so.

25. If she didn't do such a good job on something, point out what she did well.

26. After a disappointment or failure, ask, "What did you learn from the experience?"

27. When you are giving feedback, describe specific behavior. For example, "I like how you asked the question so politely" or "You still need to pick up the towels off the floor."

28. When there is a problem, focus on the issue, not the child. For example, "You didn't do the last ten problems on this assignment" is more constructive than "You never finish anything."

29. Ask what he thinks.

30. Let her be the one to choose the restaurant, movie, or activity some of the time.

31. Ask him to go with you on routine errands just because you want to spend some time with him.

32. Touch her when you talk to her.

33. Give him a hug at least every few days.

34. Go in and say goodnight before she goes to sleep. (This is easy to forget once they become teenagers.)

35. Look up and smile when he walks into the room.

36. Introduce yourself when she is with a new friend.

37. Ask her to tell you about the book she is reading or the movie she just saw.

38. Review child development literature regularly to stay updated on what is normal at each age and stage. It is important to recheck your standards and expectations to be sure they are realistic for the child's age and individual abilities.

39. Look for ways to maintain your own self-esteem. If you are unhappy, discontent, or disappointed in how your life is turning out, it will be difficult for you to build the self-esteem of your children.

40. Every child needs to be the object of a parent's undivided attention on a regular basis.

41. Make certain that your body language matches your words. If they are out of synch, he will be aware of it.

42. Be yourself. Tell the truth.

43. Be appropriate. You don't have to say everything that is on your mind or tell him things he isn't ready to know.

44. If you show that you accept yourself and your actions, you give permission to her to do the same.

Amy Morita is a licensed therapist and director of the Family Institute in Frankfurt. Call 555-0987 for your free consultation.

Counseling News

49. An Emotional Survival Guide for Teens

By Mary Tulini

This month's newsletter is written for teens. If you are a teen, this is for you. If you know a teenager, pass it along.

This month, we will explore the hardest things about being a teen and ways to make it easier on yourself. We will talk about why life is such an emotional challenge at times, and what you can do to make it less stressful. With the strategies we'll be talking about, you may even *enjoy* your teen years.

The following strategies can help you survive your teen years.

1. *Understand what emotional changes to expect.* It always helps to know what you're getting into. When you know what to expect, the changes of adolescence don't come as such a surprise. It's like seeing the trailer before you see the movie, or reading the table of contents before you start a book. It gives you a sense of what's to come, so you feel prepared.

2. *Get to know yourself better.* The teen years can be very confusing. You often may feel like you're not the same person you were when you got up this morning. How do you keep track of your changing self? One way is to keep a journal, a private notebook where you write about your feelings.

3. *Look for positive influences.* The teen years can be less stressful if you have a role model. This means someone whom you would consider a mentor, a good example, or someone to pattern yourself after. Role models are important because they set an example for you to follow. If you admire someone and model yourself after him or her, it can give you some direction and some goals. Think about the people who are positive influences in your life. They might be family members, teachers, leaders, or famous people you will never meet but whom you admire just the same.

4. *Practice thinking for yourself.* It is a sign of strong self-esteem. It means that you know you matter, and that you value your ability to think. Thinking for yourself means that you ask questions, rather than just accepting what people tell you.

5. *Learn to be assertive.* Assertive behavior is another sign of self-esteem. It usually means that a person values him- or herself.

Assertiveness is standing up for yourself and protecting your own interests.

6. *Learn to present yourself with confidence.* Here is one way to develop confidence. First, make a list of at least five things you do well. Then make a list of at least five things you *don't* do very well. Choose something to do from the first list every day. This will make you feel good about yourself. Then, when you're feeling good, do something from the second list. You will see that the way you feel about yourself at the moment can greatly affect how you perform.

7. *Learn to express your opinions.* Here are some tips:
  a. Know what you want to say. Organize your facts and arguments.
  b. Choose the best moment. Having good timing can make a huge difference in the impact your statement makes.
  c. Look friendly. People will be more receptive to you if you smile.
  d. Develop your listening skills.
  e. Watch your voice. Speak clearly and not too loudly.
  f. Disagree in a pleasant and polite way. Being rude or unfriendly turns people off and lessens your impact.
  g. Know the difference between facts and opinions. Facts will help you win your argument.
  h. Acknowledge the other point of view. People may not agree with you. You have more power when you acknowledge that others have a right to a different point of view.

8. *Find out what you believe in.* One of the tasks of adolescence is to find out what you believe in, what you value in life. This process involves questioning the ideas of people around you, especially your parents. It is understandable that you will reject some of the values and beliefs of your parents, but there are constructive ways of disagreeing.

9. *Learn to disagree productively.* There are plenty of nonproductive ways to disagree with parents and other authority figures, such as temper tantrums, violent behavior, rebellious behavior, and disobeying laws. You will have more success if you learn the more productive ways to disagree, such as developing your negotiation skills or by forming or joining an action group.

10. *Create your own private place.* As you grow older, you have a greater need for a private place that is all your own. You need it as a place to escape to, but also as a place where you can create your own life. At the end of adolescence, you will be an adult, ready to go out into the world. You will need to be ready to stand on your own, as an independent and responsible person. It helps if you have some things you can call your own, such as:
  a. A private space
  b. A place to play music
  c. A place to study and read
  d. A place to write down your thoughts and feelings, such as a private journal
  e. Places to meet friends
  f. Your own money
  g. Your own possessions

11. *Make a few good friends.* Making new friends takes some effort. Some people seem to make friends quite easily, while others find it difficult. It's mostly a matter of learning a few skills. See if you can develop behaviors like these:

a. Smile; appear friendly.
b. Say "Hi."
c. Ask questions.
d. Give compliments.
e. Join groups.
f. Ask for information. ("Where did you get your jacket?")
g. Be interested.

12. *Find someone you can talk to.* Just in case you hadn't noticed, adolescence can be a highly emotional time. You are learning new things every day and you are not always ready to meet the demands of social situations. It's very important to have someone you can talk to during this time. Different people can help you with different kinds of problems. The important thing is that when you start to feel stressed, it means you probably need to let it out. Look for help from people like these:

a. Parents
b. Siblings
c. Relatives
d. Minister or rabbi
e. Doctors
f. Psychotherapists
g. Police officers
h. Teachers
i. School psychologist
j. Guidance counselor
k. Your friends
l. Friends' parents
m. Neighbors

13. *Learn teamwork skills.* Being a part of a team is an important skill, and it will become even more important when you are an adult. Teamwork skills include things like these:

a. Cooperating
b. Making decisions
c. Being loyal

d. Encouraging others
e. Planning
f. Problem solving
g. Supporting
h. Trusting

The Desert Counseling Center offers many services for teens and their families. We hope the information in this newsletter is helpful to you, and we are here to assist you if you have questions.

Please pass this newsletter along to a friend. Or call (your number) to request additional copies.

Suggested Reading

Kelly, Kate, *The Complete Idiot's Guide to Parenting a Teenager.* New York: Alpha Books, 1996.

Law, Felicia, and Parker, Josephine, editors. *Growing Up: A Young Person's Guide to Adolescence.* Chippenham, Wiltshire, UK: Merlion Publishing, Ltd., 1993.

McCoy, Kathy, and Wibbelsman, Charles, *The New Teenage Body Book.* New York: Putnam, 1992.

Mary Tulini is the Clinical Director of The Desert Counseling Center in Scottsdale. Call 555-1234 for a free consultation, or visit www.ABCD.com for information about our services.

Relationship News

50. Relationship Checkup

By Rose Northrup

Most adults engage in long-term relationships, including marriage and other committed partnerships. Nearly everyone experiences difficulties in their marriage or committed relationship from time to time, but some people seem more prepared to anticipate these hard times and respond to them more skillfully than others.

The Relationship Checkup is a list of 11 points that will help you evaluate your relationship. These points are based on recent research completed separately by psychologists Judith Wallerstein and John Gottman (see Suggested Reading, last page). Check off the statements that apply to your relationship, and you will quickly gain a sense of the strengths and the opportunities for improvement.

1. People in successful, long-lasting relationships invested themselves fully in the relationship. While they have positive relationships with their parents, siblings, and other relatives, they are not overly involved with them. Some signs that you have a healthy relationship with your family (not too close, not too distant) include:

   ☐ Your families visit when invited.

   ☐ Their visits are short but satisfying.

   ☐ You speak with family members by phone, but not too often.

   ☐ Family members give advice when they are asked.

   The following are some signs that your family may be too involved in your life. This can create problems in your relationship over time.

   ☐ Your family members visit too often.

   ☐ They stay too long.

   ☐ They telephone frequently.

   ☐ They give unsolicited advice.

   ☐ They drop in unannounced.

2. People in successful relationships have their own identity as a couple. There is a feeling of both togetherness and independence in the relationship. If you have developed an identity as a couple, the following things are most likely true:

   ☐ You feel loyal toward each other.

   ☐ You listen carefully to each other.

   ☐ You know each other's histories.

   ☐ You pay attention to each other's moods and body language.

   ☐ You share your thoughts and feelings.

   ☐ You allow each other a private space and don't intrude on it.

   ☐ You respect each other as separate, autonomous people.

If you have not fully developed your sense of identity as a couple, you will recognize signs like these:

- ☐ You are sometimes disloyal toward each other.
- ☐ You don't listen carefully to each other.
- ☐ You don't know very much about each other's pasts.
- ☐ You ignore each other's moods and body language.
- ☐ You keep your thoughts and feelings to yourselves.
- ☐ You sometimes invade each other's private space.
- ☐ Even though you may live in the same house, it sometimes seems like you are living parallel lives.

3. Bringing children into a relationship changes it radically. Couples with children learn to successfully integrate them into their relationship. Positive signs include:

- ☐ You accept that there are times when you must place your own needs after the needs of your child.
- ☐ You do your best to stay in touch with each other emotionally and nurture your relationship.
- ☐ You set aside time every week for the two of you to spend time alone together.

The following signs indicate that you have not fully integrated children into your relationship:

- ☐ You resent the times when you must put your child's needs ahead of your own.

- ☐ You are overly focused on your child.
- ☐ You have lost touch with each other emotionally.
- ☐ You hardly ever find time to be alone with your partner.

4. Every relationship is challenged by crises and life transitions. Losing a job, a death in the family, a serious accident, or other significant event can test any relationship. If your relationship has successfully navigated life's crises and transitions, the following statements are most likely true:

- ☐ You never blame each other for the stress that comes with the crisis.
- ☐ You face difficult times as a team.
- ☐ You look for ways to support each other emotionally.
- ☐ You help each other keep your perspective when there is a crisis.
- ☐ You seek outside support during times of crisis (talking to friends and family, seeing a counselor, etc.).

If the crises and life transitions have done harm to your relationship, you have probably experienced the following during the difficult times:

- ☐ One partner seems to emotionally abandon the other.
- ☐ One partner blames the other.
- ☐ One partner becomes extremely angry, worried, or anxious.
- ☐ You don't seek support from people who could help you.

5. Successful relationships are safe places where anger, conflict, and differences

may safely be expressed. Each partner is allowed to have and express their own views. The following signs point to this being true:

☐ You have had serious conflicts, but you have not allowed them to damage your relationship.

☐ You respect the other person's right to stand his or her ground.

☐ You may find anger uncomfortable, but you accept that it is a part of life.

In relationships where it is *not* safe to express conflict, the following things are true:

☐ Your conflicts have harmed your relationship.

☐ You disagree about many things but never talk about them.

☐ You both try to intimidate the other into agreeing with your point of view.

☐ Anger is so uncomfortable that you avoid it.

☐ There are no limits to what you will do when you become angry.

6. Successful long-term relationships have a positive sexual component. The partners take care to protect their sexual relationship from the demands of work and family. The signs of such a relationship are:

☐ You sometimes have different levels of sexual need, but you make room for each other's changing levels of desire.

☐ You are honest with each other about your changing sexual desires and feelings.

☐ You set aside time for your sexual relationship and protect your privacy.

If a sexual relationship is less than satisfying, the following statements are true:

☐ You find it hard to talk about sex.

☐ Sex is like a battlefield.

☐ You never have time for sex.

7. Successful partners share laughter and fun times, and work to maintain their mutual interests. For example:

☐ You have fun together.

☐ You make each other laugh.

☐ You find each other interesting.

☐ You each have your own interests that you pursue on your own.

If your relationship is becoming stale, you will tend to describe it like this:

☐ You rarely have fun together anymore.

☐ You don't laugh much when you are together.

☐ You are bored with each other.

☐ You avoid spending time together.

☐ You have few shared interests.

8. Relationships that last are safe places where you can let down your guard and be vulnerable. You know you can count on the other to comfort and encourage you. If this is true, you might describe it as follows:

☐ It is okay to be vulnerable when you are with your partner.

☐ You understand each other.

☐ You encourage each other.

☐ You pay attention to each other's moods and respond when the other seems needy.

If your relationship is *not* a very safe place, the following is probably true:

- ☐ It is not safe to be needy and vulnerable in your relationship.
- ☐ You exhaust each other's emotional reserves.
- ☐ You don't pay attention to each other's moods.
- ☐ When you are worried about something, you avoid telling your partner.
- ☐ You feel worse about yourself when you are with your partner.

9. People who have successful long-term relationships stay romantic and idealistic about each other, even though they are growing older. These are some of the signs of such a relationship:

- ☐ You have good memories of when you fell in love with your partner.
- ☐ You are glad to be growing older with your partner.

If you have lost some of the romance of your relationship, you are likely to agree with these statements:

- ☐ You can hardly remember the days when the two of you first fell in love.
- ☐ Seeing your partner grow older makes you feel badly because it reminds you that you are growing older.

10. You have far more positive moments in your relationship than negative ones. Some signs of positive moments include:

- ☐ You show affection for each other.
- ☐ You apologize for the hurtful things you may say or do.

- ☐ You show each other empathy.
- ☐ You are polite to each other.

Examples of negative moments include:

- ☐ Your discussions often leave you feeling frustrated.
- ☐ You often pick on each other.
- ☐ Many of your conversations turn into arguments.
- ☐ You behave disrespectfully toward each other.
- ☐ You are physically violent with each other.

11. People in successful relationships are able to manage conflict productively. They are skilled at keeping times of discord from getting out of control. For example:

- ☐ You call a time-out when your emotions escalate.
- ☐ You know how to calm yourselves down.
- ☐ You take care to speak and listen nondefensively.
- ☐ You take care to validate the other person's point of view, even when you disagree with it.

Couples in less successful relationships allow conflict to become damaging in the following ways:

- ☐ You blame each other.
- ☐ You treat each other disrespectfully.
- ☐ You deny responsibility for your own actions.
- ☐ You become so angry that you leave or emotionally withdraw.

Number of items you checked in the non-shaded areas: _____
Number of items you checked in the shaded areas: _____

Ideally, you checked *no* items in the shaded areas. If you checked more than five, you have some opportunities to improve your relationship. As a beginning, you may wish to read one or more of the books listed in the Suggested Reading box. You may also wish to make an appointment for a free consultation with one of our professional counselors and develop a relationship-building plan. You will find additional relationship-building tips on our web site, www.ABCD.com.

Suggested Reading

Gottman, John, *The Seven Principles for Making Marriage Work,* New York, NY: Crown Publishers, 1999.

Gottman, John, *Why Marriages Succeed or Fail and How You Can Make Yours Last.* New York, NY: Fireside Books, 1994.

Wallerstein, Judith, and Blakeslee, Sandra, *The Good Marriage: How and Why Love Lasts.* New York, NY: Warner Books, 1995.

Rose Northrup is the Clinical Coordinator of Palatine Counseling Center in Palatine, MA. Call 555-1234 for your free consultation.

WorkLife News

51. How to Balance Work and Family Life

By Joette Washburn, Ph.D.

What Is Your Definition of Success?

If you want to create balance in your life, it is important to know how you define success. The following list is a place to start. Cross off those that don't seem important to you and add your own. Next, identify which of the items on your list are the most *essential* to your success definition and which items present the greatest *challenge* to you.

1. Being able to move on when a situation is no longer productive or positive
2. Being satisfied with your work situation
3. Enjoying the present, not putting off the good things until some time in the future
4. Expressing your creativity
5. Fulfilling your potential
6. Holding yourself with esteem separately from your work
7. Being authentic
8. Identifying your values and basing your choices on them
9. Managing your money well
10. Not feeling envious of others
11. Paying attention to your spiritual life
12. Spending time in fun ways away from your workplace
13. Spending time with people you cherish and enjoy
14. Taking good care of yourself
15. Understanding when to fight for something and when to give in

What would you add? Which items present the greatest challenge to you?

_____

_____

_____

_____

_____

The 80/20 Rule

The 80/20 Rule, also known as the Pareto Principle, says that 20% of what we do produces 80% of the results. Some examples of this principle are:

- 20% of the people sell 80% of the widgets.
- 20% of the salespeople earn 80% of the commission.
- 20% of the parts in your car cause 80% of the breakdowns.
- 20% of the members of an organization do 80% of the work.

The 80/20 principle can help anyone create balance in their life. Here's how:

1. Identify the times when you are *most* happy and productive (i.e., the 20% that produces the 80%) and *increase* them as much as possible.
2. Identify the times when you are *least* happy and productive (i.e., the 80% that produces the 20%), and *reduce* them as much as possible.

Your Seven Habits of Success

You have probably heard of Stephen Covey's *Seven Habits of Highly Effective People.* As you create balance in your life, think about your own list of success habits. What seven things would lead to more happiness in your life if you did them every day? Here are some ideas to get you started:

1. Do something you love doing for at least part of the day.
2. Get some physical exercise.
3. Get some mental exercise.
4. Stimulate yourself artistically.
5. Stimulate yourself spiritually.
6. Do something for someone else.
7. Do something just for fun.
8. Acknowledge yourself for something you said or did.

What ideas would you add?

_____

_____

_____

_____

_____

_____

Dealing with Workaholism

What if a person needs more than just self-help in dealing with a lack of balance in work and family life? An organization called Workaholics Anonymous can help.

Workaholics Anonymous is a 12-step recovery program similar to Alcoholics Anonymous. It is a "fellowship of individuals who share their experience, strength, and hope with each other that they may solve their common problem and help others recover from workaholism. The only requirement for membership is a desire to stop working compulsively."

How Do You Know if You Are a Workaholic?

Ask yourself these questions if you think you might be a workaholic:

1. Are you more comfortable talking about work than anything else?
2. Do you become impatient with people who do things besides work?
3. Do you believe that more money will solve the other problems in your life?
4. Do you get irritated when people ask you to stop working and do something else?
5. Do you get more energized about your work than about anything else, including your personal relationships?
6. Do you look for ways to turn your hobbies into money-making endeavors?
7. Do you often worry about the future, even when work is going well?
8. Do you take on extra work because you are concerned that it won't otherwise get done?
9. Do you take work home with you? Do you work on days off? Do you work while you are on vacation?

10. Do you think about your work while driving, falling asleep, or when others are talking?
11. Do you think that if you don't work hard you will lose your job or be considered a failure?
12. Do you work more than 40 hours in a typical week?
13. Do you work or read while you are eating?
14. Have your long hours hurt your family or other relationships?

For more information about Workaholics Anonymous, write or call: Workaholics Anonymous

World Service Organization
P.O. Box 289
Menlo Park, CA 94026-0289
(510) 273-9253

You can also learn more about this by visiting the web site of Alcoholics Anonymous, www.Alcoholics-Anonymous.org.

Please pass this newsletter along to a friend. Or call 555-0987 to request additional copies.

Suggested Reading

Ramona Adams, Herbert Otto, and Audeane Cowley, *Letting Go: Uncomplicating Your Life*. New York, NY: MacMillan, 1980.

Steven Carter and Julia Sokol, *Lives Without Balance: When You're Giving Everything You've Got And Still Not Getting What You Hoped For*. New York, NY: Villard Books, A Division of Random House, 1992.

Linda and Richard Eyre, *Lifebalance: How to Simplify and Bring Harmony to Your Everyday Life*. New York, NY: Fireside (Simon and Schuster), 1987.

Diane Fassel, *Working Ourselves to Death: The High Cost of Workaholism and the Rewards of Recovery*. New York, NY: HarperCollins, 1990.

Marlene Hunter, *Creative Scripts for Hypnotherapy*. New York, NY: Brunner/Mazel, 1994.

Richard Koch, *The 80/20 Principle: The Secret of Achieving More With Less*. New York, NY: Currency Books (Doubleday), 1998.

Joette Washburn is a licensed psychologist in Palos Hills. She specializes in working with executives and managers. Call 555-0987 for your free consultation.

Work/Life News

52. Does Your Company Need Family Therapy?

By Carol Knight, M.A.

How Companies Are Like Families

Like a family, a company is a group of people who have an ongoing relationship with one another. Companies have several things in common with families:

1. Families have distinct ways of communicating and degrees of togetherness. For example:

   - Communication may be overt or covert.
   - Relationships tend to be enmeshed (too close; overly involved) or disengaged (not at all close; uninvolved).
   - Boundaries may be described as diffuse (extreme togetherness), rigid (extreme separateness), or clear (ideal and appropriate).

2. There are unwritten rules which family members or employees must follow in order to survive and thrive in the system. For example, in an organization, the rules might be:

   - Never call the boss by her first name.
   - Always be at your desk by 8:00 A.M.
   - Never eat lunch with a person of lower status.
   - Don't place any personal items on your desk or credenza.

3. Unresolved issues from the past have an effect on current functioning and communication patterns.

   For example: After an emotional event such as a major strike, employees need time to process their feelings. Family therapy following a disruptive event like this would heal such wounds much more quickly.

Four Dynamics That We Bring to Work from Home

We learn to relate to people first in our families of origin. We learn to trust, communicate, listen, cooperate, and share before we reach our tenth birthday. When we join a company, we bring those abilities with us. And every work team in every company becomes a place where family dynamics play themselves out, for better or worse.

Every member of every work team brings the following kinds of dynamics from home:

1. A preference for independence and autonomy vs. dependence and control

   For example: Some people are most comfortable in a closely supervised work situation and prefer to have everything clearly spelled out. Others find such an atmosphere suffocating and seek an environment where they are left to their own devices.

2. The ability to recognize and respond to appropriate vs. inappropriate boundaries

For example: Some companies expect employees to demonstrate extreme loyalty and openness to those within the company. This atmosphere may feel comfortable to someone from a family with similar boundaries, but inappropriate to another person.

3. The ability to communicate with others effectively. This includes:

   • Stating opinions and expectations overtly vs. covertly
   • Demonstrating listening skills
   • Asking for clarification when needed
   • Speaking assertively
   • Showing respect for others

   Using effective communication skills requires strong self-esteem. This may be impossible for a person from a family where such communication was never modeled. A person who learned covert, aggressive, disrespectful communication patterns would not be successful in a work group where the preceding, effective behavior is expected.

4. Demonstrating the ability to trust others
   When employees do not trust one another, team functioning is threatened. Empowerment and motivation are maximized when people trust each other.

Signs of Dysfunction

How can you tell if a work group (or a family) is not healthy? Here are some signs of dysfunction:

1. **Attendance:** Excessive absenteeism and high turnover correlate to family members responding to dysfunction by becoming emotionally distant and running away.

2. **Sabotage:** When employees feel unable to express their feelings and opinions, they sometimes resort to acting them out by violating rules, sabotaging the company, or by displaying other passive-aggressive behaviors.

   For example: In a large company, an employee recently shared a confidential, sensitive memo with a friend who worked for a competitor. The memo became front-page headlines.

3. **Substance abuse:** Employees feeling excessive stress at work may respond as they would in a family, by abusing substances at work or after hours.

4. **Overachieving:** Companies with very high expectations may create employees who routinely produce miracles. This may look admirable to an outsider, but it can produce burnout among the employees. This dynamic resembles the family that looks perfect from the outside, but is in fact severely dysfunctional.

5. **Underachieving:** Employees who feel unappreciated or abused may respond by producing substandard results at work, just as such family members do at home.

   For example: Most stores today have sales associates who act as if the customer is an interruption. These employees appear to have no interest in the success of the company.

6. **Emotional or physical abuse:** In some organizations, employees are routinely subjected to emotional or even physical abuse. These are obviously examples of severe dysfunction, just as they are when they occur in a family.

   For example: There have recently been several reports of physical and emotional abuse in the military.

7. **Double bind:** Some work teams have an atmosphere in which employees feel "damned if you do and damned if you don't."

Strategies for Resolving Problems

Following an assessment, the following family therapy interventions may help the employees of a dysfunctional company relate with one another in a healthier and more productive way.

1. Teach employees the following communication and problem-solving skills:

   • How to define problems in a nonblaming way
   • How to listen with empathy
   • How to make requests assertively
   • How to brainstorm solutions

2. Help employees identify themes and company (family) myths. Explore those that may be discussed and challenged, as well as those that may not.
3. Triangulation is the process where two people side against a third. Teach employees to manage conflict by teaching them how to avoid triangulation.
4. Where a work team shows signs of being disengaged, help employees build stronger relationships and communication patterns. Use team-building techniques to accomplish this.
5. Where the system is enmeshed, help the employees strengthen boundaries and increase autonomy. Team-building exercises can be helpful here, too.
6. Teach supervisors how to manage employees more effectively through regular supervisory skills training. Just as parents benefit from parenting skills

training, supervisors need similar instruction. Supervisory training should address the following skills:

• How to demonstrate effective listening skills
• How to encourage open communication among team members
• How to empower team members by setting effective goals
• How to encourage creativity and initiative
• How to resolve conflict in a healthy and productive manner

The goal of such interventions is to energize employees by teaching them new ways to relate to one another.

Please pass this newsletter along to a friend. Or call 555-0987 to request additional copies.

Suggested Reading

Bob Nelson, *1001 Ways To Energize Employees*. New York, NY: Workman Publishing, 1997.

Fred Piercy, Douglas Sprenkle & Associates, *Family Therapy Sourcebook*. New York, NY: The Guilford Press, 1986.

Carol Knight is a licensed counselor in Westlake. She specializes in career issues and stress management. Call 555-0987 for your free consultation.

Workplace Psychology

53. How to Create a Positive Work Environment

By Rachel Barone, Ph.D.

Positive versus Negative Workplaces

We have all worked in places where we grew to dread getting up in the morning, and a few of us have had the pleasure of working for a boss who makes us feel like we can do anything. Let's take a look at the differences between a positive and a negative work environment.

Signs of a Negative Work Environment

- The boss is unfriendly.
- The boss is critical.
- There is high employee turnover.
- There is low employee morale.
- People watch the clock.
- People don't get much performance feedback.

Signs of a Positive Work Environment

- The boss demonstrates interest in the employees.
- The boss has an encouraging attitude.
- Employees like working there.
- There is evidence of company pride and loyalty.
- People know where they stand with their supervisors.

Thousands of books have been written on the subject of managing and motivating people, and as many training seminars are conducted on this subject around the world every day. And yet it's interesting that even with all of this available information, few companies succeed at creating a positive work environment. Let's see what's involved.

Four Key Skills

Creating a positive work environment is based on four key skills. They are:

1. Tell people what you expect of them.
2. Show interest in your team members.
3. Create an encouraging environment.
4. Recognize and reward good performance.

Skill #1: State Your Expectations

Telling people what you expect of them means doing the following:

- Communicating expectations clearly
- Having a specific job description
- Identifying specific performance standards
- Specifying deadlines
- Setting goals

Skill #2: Show Interest in Your Team

What behaviors convey that someone is interested in you?

- Making eye contact
- Calling you by name
- Asking your opinion
- Smiling
- Complimenting your work
- Taking your suggestions

These behaviors convey a *lack* of interest:

- Ignoring you
- Not knowing your name or not using it
- Not asking your opinion
- Ignoring your suggestions
- Not commenting on your work
- Following your suggestion, but only when heard from someone else

Such signs *discourage* productivity because they make people feel discouraged, angry, less confident, and stripped of self-esteem.

Skill #3: Create an Encouraging Environment

Most people would agree that an encouraging work environment is one where:

- Your ideas are valued.
- Creativity is encouraged.
- Risks are encouraged.
- Fun and laughter are valued.
- New ideas are rewarded.
- You feel appreciated.
- People thank you for your contributions.
- Flexibility is valued.
- You feel like part of the team.

Creating such an environment results in the following benefits to employees. You:

- Contribute more ideas.
- Feel more committed.
- Look forward to coming to work.
- Are more productive.
- Have increased self-esteem.

Creating such an environment results in the following benefits to managers and business owners:

- Less turnover
- Less sabotage
- Greater loyalty
- Easier to find employees due to good reputation
- Higher productivity

Skill #4: Recognize and Reward Good Performance

A reinforcer is anything that happens, after a behavior, that tends to increase the chances that the behavior will be repeated. Included are such things as:

- Compliments
- Smiles
- Thumbs-up gesture
- Saying "Thank you"
- Public announcement of your achievement
- Positive letter in your personnel file
- Promotion
- Time off
- Special parking space
- First choice on schedule
- Dinner with the boss
- Tickets to an event
- Extra employee discount
- Picture on the bulletin board
- Applause at a meeting

RECOGNITION GUIDELINES

1. *Describe the results you are recognizing. Be specific.* It's important to make certain the employee knows what behavior or accomplishment you are referring to.

2. *State your personal appreciation.* Say, "I appreciate it." Adding your personal appreciation makes the compliment feel more genuine.

3. *Encourage the person to continue producing such good work.* This increases the chances that the person will repeat the desirable behavior.

Suggested Reading

Bob Nelson, *1001 Ways to Reward Employees*. New York, NY: Workman Publishing Company, 1994.

Rachel Barone is a licensed psychologist in Tarzana Hills. She specializes in stress management. Call 555-0987 for your free consultation.

Practice News

54. Develop Your Personal Negotiation Skills

By Sam Walker, M.S.

 Negotiating skills can help you manage lots of different kinds of life situations, both at work and in your personal relationships. Here are a few examples of where these skills can help you build an even better life for yourself:

1. Many family situations require negotiating with others. Deciding which movie to see, planning how to spend money, choosing a vacation spot, and many other decisions work best when you have these skills.
2. Being a good negotiator enables you to get what you want more often without resorting to becoming aggressive or pushy. Negotiating with others is more effective than simply demanding what you want or just caving in.
3. You will be more successful in the workplace if you know how to negotiate. These skills enable you to stand up for yourself and get what you want more often without harming relationships with bosses and coworkers.
4. Negotiation skills increase your personal effectiveness in any group situation, such as volunteer groups, the PTO, and church or synagogue groups.
5. Knowing how to negotiate lessens the chances that others will take advantage of you.
6. Negotiating a fair solution makes you feel good about yourself and increases others' respect for you.

What Successful Negotiators Do

What exactly is negotiation? It is a set of skills that anyone can learn. When researchers have observed the behavior of negotiators, they learned that the most successful negotiators do the following things:

1. **They plan ahead.** Successful negotiations are rarely spontaneous. Taking the time to analyze the situation and think through your strategy is perhaps the most important element of negotiating success. This is true whether you are negotiating an important contract for your employer or negotiating your vacation plans with your family.

    Example: Anthony wants to begin running again to get into better physical shape. He became a new father 18 months ago and has had no time to exercise. He anticipates that Belinda, his wife, will resist any discussion of his wanting to take time for himself, since the responsibilities of parenthood are so time-consuming. For a while, he avoids the subject, fearing that it will turn into an argument. Then he starts to feel angry and resentful. He decides to negotiate with Belinda and begins by making a list of his needs and wants, as well as her needs and wants.

2. **They are willing to consider a wide range of outcomes and options** rather than rigidly insisting on a specific result. Negotiators who are most successful are open-minded and avoid being locked in to one outcome. They are willing to consider many possibilities and combinations of options.

   Example: Lisa is feeling very stressed by the long commute to her job. She was thinking of resigning until she decided to make a list of other options. She came up with several alternatives: working from home two days a week, working part-time rather than full-time, working flexible hours to avoid rush hour traffic, and working from home every fourth week.

3. **They look for common ground rather than areas of conflict.** Pointing out areas where you and the other person are already in agreement conveys an attitude of cooperation and lessens any feeling of opposition.

   Example: Sandy wants her next car to be a Volvo because of their reputation for safety. George wants a sports car. She says, "Let's talk about what we agree on. First, we both agree that the car has to have a strong safety record. Second, we want to buy a new car, not a used one like last time. And third, we've set our price range as $40,000 or less."

4. **They discuss the key issues in order of priority.** Have a clear idea of what the

two or three key issues are and which is the most important. Start with the most important issues and proceed to those that matter less. If you can reach agreement on the most important things, the lesser issues will most likely be easier to resolve.

   Example: Carol wants her next family vacation to be something really special— either a Caribbean cruise or a trip to San Francisco. She and her family have visited relatives or stayed at home for the past few years. She wants the family to have an experience they will always remember before Todd, their adolescent son, grow ups and moves away. She sees the key issues as follows: (1) There are only three years left before Todd leaves. He is not likely to join us for a vacation after he finishes school; (2) It is important to have an exceptional vacation at least once in your life; (3) If we plan ahead and save the money, we will be able to afford the cost of such a trip.

5. **Skillful negotiators avoid behavior that the other person is likely to consider annoying.** This includes any of the following kinds of behavior: having an aggressive or intimidating manner, using sarcasm, using negative body language, or talking loudly. Not only do skilled negotiators avoid such behavior, they work hard at conveying an attitude of cooperation, reasonableness, openness, and friendliness.

   Example: Jed is negotiating the details of his new job with his new employer in the Chicago area. When Jed moves from Memphis to Chicago to begin work, he wants Sarah, his new boss, to give him three paid days off to get settled in his new apartment. Sarah is resisting the idea. Jed says, "I thought you would be more understanding about what it takes to get settled. A reasonable person would see that this is a small request." This sarcastic remark is likely to create some doubts in Sarah's mind rather than convince her to give Jed what he wants.

6. **Good negotiators avoid participating in a defend/attack spiral.** You know what this sounds like:

A attacks B
B defends herself and attacks A
A defends herself and attacks B
B defends herself and attacks A

We've all experienced being caught in one of these spirals and know how nonproductive they are. Rather than perpetuating such a process, the successful negotiator puts a stop to it by choosing not to say anything that would be perceived as aggressive or defensive.

Example A

Jim: "I can't believe you are being so rigid."
Anne: "Rigid! You should talk! You are completely bull-headed."

Jim: "Right! You should try listening to yourself. You are impossible."

Example B

Jim: "I can't believe you are being so rigid."
Anne: "You're not happy with what I've asked for."
Jim: "You're damn right! You have to consider what I want."
Anne: "Tell me more about it, then. I'll be happy to listen."

In example A, Jim and Anne dig themselves in deeper with each statement. In example B, Anne blocks the defend/attack spiral and makes it possible for communication to resume.

With practice, you can learn to use these simple skills to get more of what you want in life—without coming across like a bully. In fact, these skills help you reach agreements that are more likely to satisfy both parties while maintaining a positive relationship. Try them in your work life or at home—they work equally well in either setting.

Sam Walker is a licensed counselor in Wauconda. He has been in private practice for 24 years and specializes in working with people with terminal illnesses. Call 555-0987 for your free consultation.

Manager Updates

55. How to Give Effective Performance Feedback

By Cassandra Jolie, M.S.

Consequences of *Not* Giving Effective Feedback

Let's take a look at some typical examples of what goes on in work environments when managers *don't* give good feedback.

Example #1: John has been working at his new job for one month. On his first day at work, Wilma, his boss, showed him what to do and got him started on a project. Since then, Wilma has communicated with him mostly through voice mail and e-mail. She walks past his cubicle and says hello a few times each day, but there hasn't been much other communication. John is assuming he is doing his job properly, but he really isn't sure.

Analysis: There is no feedback here. John has no idea whether he is doing his job properly.

Solution: Wilma should have given John a detailed job description on the first day. She should have gone over his first project as soon as he finished it, making certain he understood the task and completed it properly. She also should have checked in with him regularly to make certain he was doing his job correctly and to see whether he had any questions.

Example #2: Stella works in an office. Yesterday, she spent several hours filing a huge stack of folders that her boss had given her in the morning. When she got to work today, her boss came over to her desk and yelled, "Stella! You did those files all wrong! Don't you *listen?*" He said it so loudly that Stella's three office mates turned toward her in shock. He went back into his office and slammed the door.

Analysis: This manager's behavior is abusive. It lowers her self-esteem and frightens her coworkers. An atmosphere of fear also lowers productivity and encourages sabotage and turnover.

Solution: He should have delivered the feedback calmly and in private. He should also have asked her for her understanding of the task; perhaps there was a reason for it being done the way it was. Third, he should have been specific about what she did wrong.

Example #3: Angela asked Steve, her assistant, to call a list of 20 clients and set up phone interviews for *next* Thursday and Friday (the 20th and 21st). She provided Steve with an updated list of phone numbers and told him the hours she would be available to speak with the clients. When Angela came back from lunch today, Steve had left a list of interviews on her desk. He has set them up for *this* Thursday and Friday (the 13th and 14th). He also has written, next to four of the clients' names, "wrong phone number." As she picks up the phone to reschedule the first client, she says to herself, "See, you just can't get good help these days."

Analysis: As far as we can tell, there was no feedback to this employee.

Solution: Employees have a hard time learning if they are not given feedback. This manager should have talked to Steve calmly and in private. She should also have asked Steve what he understood the task to be and why he scheduled the interviews for the wrong dates. Finally, she should have asked Steve to reschedule the calls for the correct dates.

Steps for Giving Feedback

Now that we've looked at a few examples of what can happen when performance feedback *isn't* given effectively, let's talk about some principles for doing it well. The five simple steps are:

1. Describe the situation.
2. Ask the employee for his or her view of the situation.
3. Come to an understanding of the situation.
4. Develop an action plan to resolve the situation.
5. Agree to follow up later to make certain the situation has been resolved.

Let's use the third example above to illustrate how this might look.

1. *Describe the situation.* "Steve, these appointments are all scheduled for the 13th and 14th. I asked you to schedule them for the 20th and 21st."
2. *Ask the employee for his or her view of the situation.* "Tell me, what was your understanding of what I asked you to do?"
3. *Come to an understanding of the situation.* "So you just misunderstood what I wanted. I had written the dates in my note to you, but you didn't read it thor-

oughly before you started making the calls."
4. *Develop an action plan to resolve the situation.* "I would like you to re-schedule all of these appointments before 5:00 today. What will it take for you to do that?"
5. *Agree to follow up later to make certain the situation has been resolved.* "I'll check in with you at 4:30 to see how you are doing with this." At 4:30, stop by Steve's desk and ask, "How are you doing on your calls?"

Principles for Giving Feedback

Let's take a look at some other issues to consider when giving feedback to someone who works on your team.

1. **Put it in writing.** Feedback is most effective when it is written down. Having it in writing increases the chances that it will be understood. For example, Angela could simply note the dates and times she is available and hand it to Steve. She could also write "by 5 P.M. today" at the top.
2. **Be sensitive to people's feelings.** Some managers think they don't need to worry about the employee becoming upset. They think that as the boss, they have the right to tell people what to do and not worry about their feelings. This is a big mistake. Being concerned about other people's feelings is important in any situation. Effective managers demonstrate concern for the self-esteem of their team members. This doesn't mean withholding criticism or ignoring problems.
3. **Focus on your entire team, not just the new members.** New employees are not

the only ones who need performance feedback. *All* employees need ongoing feedback.

4. **Feedback should be as specific as possible.** People have a difficult time responding to instructions that are vague and unclear. It is important to check for understanding; avoid assuming that you are on the same wavelength.

5. **Think it through.** Always take the time to plan what you want to say before giving feedback. Taking the time to gather your thoughts and clarify what you want your feedback to accomplish increases the chances that you will communicate clearly.

6. **Ask first.** Get the employee's point of view *before* you state what you think should be done. People are more receptive when they have a chance to explain themselves first. You might also learn something unexpected that will explain the situation or change your point of view.

7. **Don't withhold.** It is not a good idea to hold back your negative observations when employees are new. You don't want to criticize too much and cause them to feel discouraged, but remember that people need to know how they are doing.

8. **Follow up.** If you see that the employee corrected a problem situation, you still need to follow up. When you follow up, you are telling employees that you are being thorough and that the work is important.

Please pass this newsletter along to a friend. Or call 555-0987 to request additional copies.

Cassandra Jolie is a licensed counselor in West Payton. She specializes in working with executives and managers on workplace issues, stress management, etc. Call 555-0987 for your free consultation.

Practice News

56. How to Manage Conflict at Work

By Peter Cohen, MSW

Kinds of Workplace Conflicts

Let's start by identifying where conflicts happen. Think about the kinds of conflicts that happen around your workplace.

- Disagreements over turf (who should do what)
- Disagreements over policy (how things should be done)
- Conflicts of personality and style

Common Ways of Dealing with Conflict

These are some of the ways we typically deal with conflict. Do you see yourself in any of them?

- Avoid the conflict.
- Deny the conflict; wait until it goes away.
- Change the subject.
- React emotionally; become aggressive, abusive, hysterical, or frightening.
- Find someone to blame.
- Make excuses.
- Delegate the situation to someone else.

All of these responses are nonproductive. Some of them are actually destructive. This is why learning to manage conflict is so important.

Effect on Work Relationships

The workplace is a system of relationships. Relationships have many different aspects; here are several examples:

Trust
Teamwork
Quality
Morale
Self-esteem
Loyalty
Respect for boss

When conflicts are handled well, there's a positive effect on work relationships. When they are not, these factors can deteriorate. Productivity and the free expression of ideas are also impacted.

Factors That Affect How People Manage Conflict

The skills involved in managing conflict are learned behaviors. None of us is born knowing how to deal with differences of opinion, arguments, or turf wars. Some of the factors that affect how we behave in the face of conflict are:

1. **Status:** People in higher-status positions usually feel freer to engage in conflict and are less likely to avoid confrontation.
2. **Company style or unwritten rules:** Some companies encourage conflict; others have unwritten rules that it is to be contained or avoided.
3. **Gender differences:** Males are generally encouraged to be more confrontational than females.
4. **Behavior learned in families:** In some families, conflict and confrontation are a communication style. In others, conflict always remains hidden.
5. **Behavior learned from role models:** People who have had a teacher or boss who modeled effective conflict-resolution skills are more likely to develop these skills themselves.

Conflict Resolution Skills

No one is born knowing how to resolve conflicts. Conflict resolution is a set of skills that anyone can learn. Let's look at two important ones: active listening and conflict deescalation skills.

Active Listening

Active listening is a valuable skill for resolving conflicts because it enables you to

demonstrate that you understand what another person is saying and how he or she is feeling about it. Active listening means restating, in your own words, what the other person has said.

Active listening is a way of checking whether your understanding is correct. It also demonstrates that you are listening and that you are interested and concerned. These all help resolve a situation when there are conflicting points of view.

Active listening responses have two components: (1) naming the feeling that the other person is conveying, and (2) stating the reason for the feeling.

Here are some examples of active-listening statements:

"Sounds like you're upset about what happened at work."
"You're annoyed by my lateness, aren't you?"
"You sound really stumped about how to solve this problem."
"It makes you angry when you find errors on Joe's paperwork."
"Sounds like you're really worried about Wendy."
"I get the feeling you're awfully busy right now."

Actively listening is *not* the same as agreement. It is a way of demonstrating that you intend to hear and understand another's point of view.

Benefits of Active Listening

If a person uses active listening as part of his or her communication style at work, how would that be good for resolving conflicts, i.e., what are the benefits?

1. It feels good when another person makes an effort to understand what you are thinking and feeling. It creates good feelings about the other person and makes you feel better about yourself.
2. Restating what you've heard, and checking for understanding, promotes better communication and produces fewer misunderstandings.
3. Responding with active listening has a calming effect in an emotional situation.

Conflict Deescalation

Everyone has been in an argument that has escalated. Before you know it, it's blown out of proportion. Let's think for a moment about some actions that will help you deescalate a conflict. In your experience, what actions put a stop to the defend/attack spiral?

- Stick with "I" statements; avoid "you" statements.
- Avoid name-calling and put-downs ("A reasonable person could see that . . .").

- Soften your tone.
- Take a time-out ("Let's take a break and cool down").
- Acknowledge the other person's point of view (agreement is not necessary).
- Avoid defensive or hostile body language (rolling eyes, crossing arms in front of body, tapping foot).
- Be specific and factual; avoid generalities.

Conflict Prevention Skills

Now that we've talked about how to resolve a conflict, let's look at how to prevent conflicts from happening. Here are a few ideas:

- Bring issues out in the open before they become problems.
- Be aware of triggers and respond to them when you notice them.
- Have a process for resolving conflicts. Bring it up at a meeting and get agreement on what people should do in cases of differing viewpoints.
- Teach everyone conflict-resolution skills and expect people to use them.

Peter Cohen is a licensed Clinical Social Worker in Forest Hills. He specializes in workplace issues. Call 555-0987 for your free consultation.

Mental Health News

57. How to Recover from a Career Crisis

By Alice Kim, M.S.

If you have ever experienced any of the following, you have had a career crisis:

- Losing your job
- Being fired
- Burning out
- Not wanting to do your job for one more day

A career crisis can be caused either by someone else (being laid off) or by your own feelings (burning out).

Common Causes of Career Crises

There are many reasons why people experience career crises. Here are a few:

- Corporate downsizing
- Burnout
- Relocating for your spouse's career
- Being fired
- Making the wrong career move
- Corporate politics
- Not fitting in

Why a Career Crisis Is So Devastating

A career crisis is almost always devastating because it can impact your life in so many ways. Here are a few examples:

1. **Money:** Losing your income with no warning can be financially devastating.
2. **Status:** If your job gives you status or a professional identity, you may feel devastated without it.
3. **Surprise:** If the job loss happens without warning, you will probably feel shocked.
4. **Self-esteem:** You may feel embarrassed by what has happened.
5. **Feeling alone:** You are likely to lose friends and companions when you no longer work in the same place.
6. **Feeling out of synch:** Your regular routine may be disrupted.
7. **Confusion:** If the crisis happens because of burnout or for reasons inside yourself, you may feel confused about what to do next.
8. **Effect on others:** If people around you depend on your income and need you to be predictable, they may react negatively to your crisis.

Career Crisis: Who It Hurts the Most

A career crisis hurts *you* because it is devastating to your ego. The hurt tends to be greater when one gets a sense of identity and self-esteem from his or her job title, status, and income.

A crisis hurts *your family* because they must experience the emotional fallout that follows a crisis. Your family may also experience a feeling of lost self-esteem and status, especially if you were fired or laid off.

The Flashback Effect

A major loss like this sometimes can cause you to reach back into the past and reactivate unfinished business from a major loss, or a crisis from an earlier time.

For example, when Sharon was terminated after seven months at her dream job, she became very depressed. While depression is a normal reaction to such a loss, Sharon was reacting to losing her job *and* the similar feelings she had when she flunked out of a top university 12 years earlier. When she finally saw a therapist after a few weeks of depression following the job loss, she saw that she had never fully resolved her feelings about failing in college.

Here are some other points about recovery:

1. The process of recovering from a career crisis will happen on its own schedule. It can't be rushed.
2. Every person responds to a career crisis differently. There is no right way to respond or to deal with it.
3. Depending on the circumstances, processing a career crisis can take years.
4. Build and use a support system. People need other people when they are experiencing such a crisis. A group of people who have experienced similar losses is especially helpful.
5. It is a good idea to find support outside of your family and friends. Even the most supportive may grow tired of hearing about your situation, or you may find yourself censoring your behavior to avoid alienating them. However, you still need help and a place to let your feelings out.

How to Help Someone in a Career Crisis

Here are a few ideas for being helpful to people going through career crises:

1. People need support when they are having a career crisis, even though they may seem to push you away.
2. Ask how you can help.
3. Don't give advice unless asked.
4. Check in regularly with the crisis victim; let him or her know you're there.
5. Remind the crisis victim of what a good person he or she is, even without the identity and status that the job provided.
6. Sometimes a career crisis sends a person into a serious depression for which help is needed. If you sense danger, urge the crisis victim to seek help.

How to Turn a Crisis into a Victory

Here are some suggestions for turning a career crisis into a victory:

1. Give yourself time to heal. If recovery is rushed or interrupted, the crisis victim will not fully heal and a victory is not possible.

2. Remind yourself as often as necessary that your pain will end and you will eventually feel happy again.

3. Avoid jumping into something new on the rebound; let yourself experience all the stages of grief.

4. Accept that many people will not understand the depth of your grief. They will not understand why this is so difficult for you, and they will say stupid things.

5. Use the opportunity to stop and consider other options.

6. Explore what meaning your feelings have for you. If we pay attention to them, our feelings can lead us places we would otherwise never visit.

7. Keep a journal of your experiences. Make it your intention to see what there is to be learned from this experience.

8. A loss such as a career crisis can be viewed as both a door-closer and a door-opener. Start thinking about what you are learning and gaining from this experience.

9. Create a ceremony of letting go. Yours will be as unique as your experience.

The Career Crisis Recovery Exercise

Write out your answers to the following questions. This self-help exercise can help you process your feelings about what has happened to you.

1. Describe what happened when your career crisis happened.

2. Describe the job or career. Where did you work? What was it like? Who did you work with? What do you miss the most? What do you not miss at all?

3. Describe your feelings about the loss of the job or career.

4. What has the impact of this crisis been on your life? What else have you lost because of your career crisis?

5. What barriers stop you from moving on?

6. What are 10 things you can do starting today to continue the recovery process?

Please pass this newsletter along to a friend. Or call 555-0987 to request additional copies.

Suggested Reading

William Bridges, *Job Shift: How To Prosper In A Workplace Without Jobs.* Reading, MA: Addison-Wesley, 1994.

Barry Glassner, *Career Crash: The New Crisis—and Who Survives.* New York: Simon and Schuster, 1994.

Ayala Pines and Elliot Aronson, *Career Burnout: Causes and Cures.* New York: The Free Press, 1988.

Alice Kim is a licensed counselor in Schaumburg. She specializes in working with adults and families. Call 555-0987 for a consultation.

Work/Life Update

58. Should You Leave Your Job?

By Susan Backus, D.S.W.

Most of us have to work for a living. Since we spend so many hours each week at our jobs, it's very important that there is a good fit. If you have been feeling less enthusiastic about your work situation recently, maybe you have even begun to wonder if it is time to move on.

Here are seven signs that your job is no longer the right one for you.

1. **You no longer look forward to going to work in the morning.** This may seem obvious, but many people overlook it because it happens gradually. Think about how you felt when you first started working at your company. Most people feel pretty excited about their work in the beginning, looking forward to each day and thinking about the projects they will be working on. It's normal for that enthusiasm to tone down somewhat, but if you notice that you are feeling bored, indifferent, or actually wish you didn't have to go,

maybe it's time for a change. This is especially true if you're spending 60 hours a week at your job, which is not unusual in today's workplace. You owe it to yourself to do something that gives you satisfaction.

Try to identify what part of your work situation is bothering you. Distinguish between the aspects that you can fix and the things that you can do nothing about. If you can figure out how to spend more time on the job doing things that you enjoy, you may once again find yourself more eager to get to work in the morning.

2. **You have lowered your standards.** Most of us take pride in our work and our careers, and therefore set high standards for ourselves. If you have begun to allow yourself to turn in work that's just good enough to get the job done, you have let your standards slide. This is dangerous because when you compromise your personal standards, your self-esteem will fall.

To remedy this problem, think about why it is happening. Maybe this kind of work no longer presents a challenge to you. If that is true, identify the types of projects that will get you excited. Perhaps you can volunteer for assignments outside your department. But if you can't figure out a way to jump-start your job, you may want to start thinking about a change.

3. **You have lower self-esteem.** If you no longer receive praise or acknowledgment for your work, it's normal both to wonder if the

company no longer values you and to second-guess your own abilities. If you feel like you can discuss this with your boss, do so. Ask for specific feedback about your performance. You will either learn that you are more valued than you thought, or you will find out what you need to work on.

Another option is to talk with a trusted coworker or with someone who knows your boss's leadership style. Maybe he or she gives people feedback only when there is a problem. Some supervisors don't understand that people need feedback when things are going well, not just when there is a problem. If this is true, you will have to decide whether you want to stay with a boss who keeps you in the dark. It may be worth it for you to stay where you are, since most bosses eventually move on.

4. **Your supervisor doesn't help you grow and develop.** Without support for career development, you will eventually reach a dead end. There are a number of ways this may be evident. Perhaps you ask to attend professional conferences (including inexpensive local ones), but your requests are turned down because there are no budget dollars available. Or you are not allowed to participate in cross-functional teams that would enable you to develop new skills. These blocked opportunities may happen because your boss may feel threatened, or he or she

may fear losing you if you develop too many skills. In some cases, the boss just doesn't know how to develop people.

You may not have to leave your job to solve this problem. You can make a decision to manage your own career development. Take classes on your own time. Join a professional association and attend their meetings. Do everything you can to keep growing. Eventually, of course, if your boss continues to limit you, you will feel the effects on the job and you will have to decide when it is time to move on.

5. **You get stuck with low-profile assignments.** This happens to everyone at one time or another. It may be a one-time situation, where somebody needs to do the project, and it's your turn. But what happens when one dead-end assignment follows another? This could become a problem if you feel like you are drifting along with a series of these projects. This could be a sign that you are perceived as less competent and less valuable.

If you think it is not too late to turn things around, then resolve to regain control of your place in the organization. Talk to your boss about what you want to do next. Ask what you need to do to participate in more challenging projects. Listen to your boss's feedback and do what is suggested.

6. **You have been pigeonholed.** It is not uncommon to become identified with your first position or with a project that you managed earlier in your career. Even though you learn new skills and get promoted, people may associate you with your previous experiences. This happens often to people who start their careers in hourly or administrative jobs and earn promotions to management levels. Even though you are no longer a secretary,

you are still asked to take minutes at the manager's meeting. The challenge is to find a way out of the pigeonhole and keep your career from being stalled.

To resolve this problem, ask your boss to give you a chance to do a special project that will change the way people see you. This could be a unique assignment that will require just a small percentage of your time during a specified period. Offer to do the assignment as a test, and be sure to guarantee that you will do the rest of your job in a satisfactory way. If the project is successful, both you and the company will benefit. If your boss agrees to this project, you may be able to move beyond the role you have been typecast in. If not, you will have to decide whether you want to stay with the department or the company.

7. **You no longer respect the company you work for.** Most people want to be proud of the organization they work for. When you

tell others what you do and you don't mention the company's name, that's not a good sign. It could mean that your values are no longer in synch with the company's values, and this is making you feel very uncomfortable. If this is the case, and if it is unlikely to change, the best strategy may be to begin to look for an employer who shares your values.

Susan Backus is a Licensed Clinical Social Worker in Springfield. She specializes in helping people with work and career issues. Call 555-0987 for your free consultation.

About the CD-ROM

Introduction

The files on the enclosed CD-ROM are saved in Microsoft Word for Windows version 7.0. In order to use the forms, you will need to have word processing software capable of reading Microsoft Word for Windows version 7.0 files.

System Requirements

- IBM PC or compatible computer
- CD-ROM drive
- Windows 95 or later
- Microsoft Word for Windows version 7.0 (including the Microsoft converter*) or later or other word processing software capable of reading Microsoft Word for Windows 7.0 files.

*Word 7.0 needs the Microsoft converter file installed in order to view and edit all enclosed files. If you have trouble viewing the files, download the free converter from the Microsoft web site. The URL for the converter is:

http://office.microsoft.com/downloads/2000/wrd97cnv.aspx

Microsoft also has a viewer that can be downloaded, which allows you to view, but not edit documents. This viewer can be downloaded at:

http://office.microsoft.com/downloads/9798/wd97vwr32.aspx

NOTE: Many popular word processing programs are capable of reading Microsoft Word for Windows 7.0 files. However, users should be aware that a slight amount of formatting might be lost when using a program other than Microsoft Word.

Using the Files

Loading Files

To use the word processing files, launch your word processing program. Select **File, Open** from the pull-down menu. Select the appropriate drive and directory. A list of files should appear. If you do not see a list of files in the directory, you need to select **WORD DOCUMENT (*.DOC)** under **Files of Type**. Double click on the file you want to open.

Printing Files

If you want to print the files, select **File, Print** from the pull-down menu.

User Assistance

If you need assistance or if you have a damaged CD-ROM, please contact Wiley Technical Support at:

Phone: (212) 850-6753
Fax: (212) 850-6800 (Attention: Wiley Technical Support)
URL: www.wiley.com/techsupport

CD-ROM Contents

Folder: General Topics

Newsletter 1	33 Ways to Use Your Journal for Self-Discovery and Self-Expression	Newsletter1.doc
Newsletter 2	Addiction: How to Recognize It and What to Do about It	Newsletter2.doc
Newsletter 3	Why Am I So Anxious?	Newsletter3.doc
Newsletter 4	Assertive Communication: 20 Tips	Newsletter4.doc
Newsletter 5	Depression: What It Is and What to Do about It (Part I)	Newsletter5.doc
Newsletter 6	Depression: What It Is and What to Do about It (Part II)	Newsletter6.doc
Newsletter 7	How People Change	Newsletter7.doc
Newsletter 8	How to Be More Self-Confident	Newsletter8.doc
Newsletter 9	How to Have More Self-Esteem	Newsletter9.doc
Newsletter 10	When Should You Consult a Mental Health Professional?	Newsletter10.doc
Newsletter 11	Dealing with Midlife Issues	Newsletter11.doc
Newsletter 12	Simplify Your Life	Newsletter12.doc
Newsletter 13	Keeping Anger under Control	Newsletter13.doc
Newsletter 14	Letting Go of the Past	Newsletter14.doc
Newsletter 15	Caring for the Caregiver	Newsletter15.doc
Newsletter 16	Moving beyond Grief and Loss	Newsletter16.doc
Newsletter 17	Managing Perfectionism	Newsletter17.doc
Newsletter 18	How to Be Less of a Perfectionist and Enjoy Life More	Newsletter18.doc
Newsletter 19	What Makes You Procrastinate?	Newsletter19.doc
Newsletter 20	How to Stop Procrastinating	Newsletter20.doc
Newsletter 21	Recovering from Sexual Assault	Newsletter21.doc
Newsletter 22	What to Do about the Holiday Blues	Newsletter22.doc
Newsletter 23	What Causes All of This Stress?	Newsletter23.doc

CD-ROM Contents

Folder: Marriage and Family

Folder: Work and Career

CD-ROM Contents

For information about the CD-ROM see the **About the CD-ROM** section on page 187.

WILEY
Publishers Since 1807